Memoirs of Mary A. Maverick

MARY A. MAVERICK AND CHILDREN

Memoirs

of

Mary A. Maverick

arranged by

Mary A. Maverick

and her son

Geo. Madison Maverick

Edited by

Rena Maverick Green

Introduction by Sandra L. Myres

University of Nebraska Press
Lincoln and London

First Bison Book printing: 1989
Most recent printing indicated by the first digit below:
1   2   3   4   5   6   7   8   9   10

Library of Congress Cataloging-in-Publication Data
Maverick, Mary Adams.
    Memoirs of Mary A. Maverick / arranged by Mary A. Maverick
and her son Geo. Madison Maverick; edited by Rena Maverick Green;
introduction by Sandra L. Myres.
    p.   cm.
    Reprint. Originally published: San Antonio, Tex.: Alamo Printing
Co., c1921.
    ISBN 0-8032-3136-9 (alk. paper).   ISBN 0-8032-8159-5 (pbk.: alk.
paper)
    1. Maverick, Mary Adams. 2. Pioneers—Texas—Biography.
3. Women pioneers—Texas—Biography. 4. Frontier and pioneer
life—Texas. 5. Texas—History—1846–1950.   I. Maverick, Geo.
Madison (George Madison) II. Green, Rena Maverick. III. Title.
F391.M466   1989   88-31141
976.4'009'94—dc 19   CIP

Reprinted from the 1921 edition published by the Alamo Printing
Co., San Antonio, Texas

DEDICATION.

There are twelve of us in all, my husband and I, and ten children—six living and six in the Spirit-land.

To the memory of the dear ones who have gone before, I dedicate these reminiscences of by-gone years.

MARY A. MAVERICK

Contents

INTRODUCTION BY SANDRA L. MYRES

In a 1969 article, historian Robert Utley commented that many of the army wives' journals could be considered "minor frontier classics."[1] He might have extended that statement beyond army wives to other women who lived and wrote about their frontier experiences. Since Utley's article appeared, frontierswomen's journals, diaries, reminiscences, and letters have been "discovered" by historians. A whole new frontier history and literature, written from a female, and sometimes a very feminist standpoint, has emerged. The two best-known Texas women's books are those of Mary Ann Adams Maverick and Sallie Reynolds Matthews, both listed in John H. Jenkins's *Basic Texas Books: An Annotated Bibliography of Selected Works for a Research Library.*[2]

Maverick was eighty-two in 1896 when she assembled and published her memoirs with the assistance of her son, George Madison Maverick. The volume was put together from her diaries, notes, and correspondence and was evidently intended for only a few family members. According to Maverick's granddaughter, Rena Maverick Green, only five or six copies of this early version were printed. None appear to have survived. In 1921 Green, recognizing the importance of the memoirs to Texas history, edited and prepared them for more extensive distribution through the Alamo Printing Company of San Antonio. Green later published *Samuel Maverick Texan, 1803–1870: A Collection of Letters, Journals and Memoirs* (1952), which incorporated Mary Maverick's memoirs along with a "wealth of extracts from letters, diaries and journals of Samuel Maverick."[3] However, it is Green's 1921 edition of Mary Maverick's memoirs that are reprinted in this volume. The only change made from the 1921 edition has been to correct a printing error on pages 63 and 69 which plunged the reader into narrative chaos.[4] It is an extremely rare and much-sought-after item by libraries and collectors of Texana and indeed of United States frontier history. Thus, the present reprint is particularly welcome.

Unfortunately, historians have often misinterpreted both the meaning and significance of women's diaries and memoirs. Mary Maverick's memoirs are an excellent example. First, the memoirs are both myth and history. They tell us a good deal about women on the frontier, how they lived and how they coped. However, they must be read in the context of what the Mavericks wanted, and did not want, known. First, one needs to consider why Mary wrote her memoirs. There are two answers, one in the preface, the other in the appendix. As Mary wrote in the preface, she hoped the book would "be of use in cementing my descendants together in the distant future, as they are now united in the spirit of kindly kinship." The second reason is clear from the appendix (beginning on page 117), where Mary attempted to clear her husband's name from its connection with the branding of other people's cattle—a piece of Texas folklore (true or untrue) that persists to the present day.

To really understand what life was like for women in ninetennth-century Texas the *Memoirs of Mary A. Maverick* should be read in conjunction with several other Texas women's books, especially those of her close contemporaries Mary Crownover Rabb and Teresa Vielé[5] and later, but still relevant, *Interwoven: A Pioneer Chronicle* by Sallie Reynolds Matthews.[6] Pieced together from diaries, letters, and memory, Maverick's work is not as coherent nor as well written as either Matthews's or Vielé's books. However, it is longer, easier to read, and more complete in detail than the Rabb diary, which was written phonetically in a penciled copy that was never finished and was not published until 1962.[7]

There are what have been called "archetypical" pioneer reminiscences. These contain what is "expected" in pioneer stories, such as a great prairie fire, a grasshopper plague, or the "last Indian raid" in such and such a country. Maverick's memoirs are not this type of work. She may not have told the whole truth, but she did not put in things that did not happen.

Mary Ann Adams, as related in the first chapter, was born

in Tuscaloosa County, Alabama, the daughter of William Lewis Adams and Agatha Strother Lewis. She grew up on her family's plantation and received some education at Tuscaloosa Academy. On August 4, 1836, at the age of eighteen, she married Samuel Augustus Maverick, a South Carolinian fifteen years her elder who had participated in the Texas revolution and planned to make his permanent home in Texas.[8] Eventually most of the Adams family relocated in Texas. Two of Mary's brothers were already there in 1836, and she was later joined by her youngest sister, Elizabeth ("Lizzie"), who married Robert Clow. The two sisters kept up a lengthy and often very interesting correspondence, now a part of the Maverick papers at the Barker Texas History Center at the University of Texas at Austin.

When I reread Maverick's memoirs, I made a note that the first two chapters and chapter nine would be primarily of interest to genealogists and could be passed over by historians. Wrong! Maverick's sense of who she was and where she came from are critical themes in understanding her and the time in which she lived. In the nineteenth century (especially in the South, but in the rest of the country as well), family ties were important. This was true not only for socially and politically active families like the Adamses and Mavericks, but others as well. Recall, moreover, that one of Mary's reasons for writing the memoir was to "cement" her "descendants together." Thus it was important to her that her descendants know who their ancestors were and where they came from.

The third chapter of the memoirs, "Ho, For the Lone Star," will be of special interest to frontier historians interested in overland travel. For those who have read overland travel accounts, especially for the trans-Mississippi West, many parts of this chapter will seem familiar. The details of preparing for the journey, the tearful departure from family and friends, and "laying over" to wash and rest suggest similarities to the later and longer overland trips to Oregon and California. Of course, the distance the Mavericks traveled was shorter than that of later overlanders. The country was better settled, and the Mavericks traveled in some luxury with a large retinue of slaves and servants. Nonetheless, they encountered bad roads, "much mud," and areas where the country was poor and sparsely settled and "provisions for man and beast short." It is also of interest to note that many of the same conditions still existed in East Texas when Elizabeth Custer traveled through much of the same country after the Civil War.[9]

The remainder of the memoirs are an engrossing and important (albeit somewhat disconnected) description of the Mavericks' years in Texas—then considered the far western frontier. The Mavericks lived first in San Antonio. Then, during the so-called Runaway of 1842 (brought on by the rumor of an impending Mexican invasion), they fled eastward. They stayed occasionally with friends, or in temporary quarters, until they finally set up a home near Gonzales on the Colorado River. In 1844 they moved to Decrows Point on Matagorda Bay (where Sam owned considerable property) and remained there until 1847, when they returned to San Antonio. During this period of moving from place to place, Mary occasionally set up housekeeping in rather strange accommodations, including, as she related, a corn crib and a blacksmith shop. Nonetheless, they had numerous friends and acquaintances who offered them shelter and hospitality. Certainly Mary Maverick never lived, as did Mary Rabb, under a quilt spread over a tree, or "in a camp gust [sic] a few bords over us all the frunt and sids was open to the wind," or "in camp where the horse flyes and musceatoes was so bad we had to leave."[10]

Mary's early years in Texas were devoted to making a home and raising her family. She bore ten children in twenty-one years. Four died before reaching the age of eight. Although high infant mortality rates were common during this period, especially on the frontier, Mary had great difficulty in reconciling herself to the loss of her children. Both she and Sam were heartbroken by the loss of their two young daughters, Agatha and Augusta. Mary described Sam's grief and anguish following Agatha's death in some detail and noted that he finally found relief accompanying his close friend, Colonel Jack Hays, on an expedition to open a shorter trade route between San Antonio and Chihuahua, Mexico. Mary had no such opportunity for escape. Although she did not mention it in her published account, following Agatha's and Augusta's deaths she filled her private pocket diary with an outpouring of self-guilt and expressed her fears that, in some way, Sam blamed her for the girls' deaths and had ceased to love her. She increasingly sought relief and comfort from these tragedies in spiritualism and turned to homeopathic medical treatments for her other children. It should be noted, however, that such practices were fairly common in the nineteenth century and should not be considered strange or unusual behavior.[11]

One special caution about the *Memoirs*. Some of the history is not correct. For example, Mary identified the Tonkawa Indians as cannibals; they were not. She may have confused them with the Karankawas, who did practice ceremonial cannibalism and were particularly despised by early Anglo Texans.[12] Some parts of the account of the Council House Fight (described on pp. 31–37) are inaccurate, as any Texas historian can confirm.[13] However, note that Mary was only twenty-two at the time and was involved with house and children. She neither knew nor understood the background of the episode. Nonetheless, her account of the events as she witnessed them is an important piece of historical evidence. She tells us more of the events and aftermath of this infamous incident than all the academic historians who so knowingly and pontifically write from a latter-day viewpoint. Maverick's account may not be "history" as I, or any other professor of Texas history, would relate it in a classroom, but it does give us another perspective that may be more "real" for our students than "just the facts."

During much of their married life Sam and Mary were separated. Often away from home, he devoted most of his time to business, politics, and the promotion of Texas. For two months of 1842 he was a prisoner in Mexico. After he returned, he served in the Eighth Congress of the Republic of Texas. After the annexation of Texas to the United States, he served in the Texas legislature from January 1853 to November 1862.[14] Mary took care of the house and the children; Sam attended to business and politics—a domestic situation that lasted well beyond their time.

Despite their numerous children, frequent moves, and Sam's long absences from home, the Mavericks led an active social life entertaining and being entertained by some of the best-known figures in Texas, including former president of the Republic Mirabeau B. Lamar, San Antonio mayor Juan Seguin, General Alexander Somervell, and Prince Carl of Solms-Braunfels, as well as Sam's long-time friend and companion, Texas Ranger Jack Hays. Thus the *Memoirs* offer revealing insights into nineteenth-century social life.[15]

Much of Mary's reminiscence is somewhat naïve. Unlike Vielé, for example, she had little interest in, or knowledge of, politics; her major interests were her children and making a good home for them and her husband. However, as her children grew up, Mary became increasingly active in civic affairs. During the Civil War, with four sons in the army, she was active in San Antonio Confederate relief activities. She also devoted a good deal of time to church work and was one of the founders of Saint Mark's church of San Antonio and president of the Ladies' Parish Aid Society. After Sam's death in 1870, she increased her civic endeavors. She was a member of the San Antonio Historical Society and the Daughters of the Republic of Texas and for many years president of the Alamo Monument Association, which helped to protect what was left of the famous old mission.[16]

Despite the episodic nature of the writing and the occasional inaccuracies (including some in the footnotes, which were based on old and long out-of-date sources), Mary Maverick's memoirs are an important contribution not only to the history of Texas but to our understanding of women's lives in the trans-Mississippi West.

NOTES

1. Robert Utley, "Arizona Vanquished: Impressions and Reflections Concerning the Quality of Life on a Military Frontier," *American West* 6 (November 1969): 16.

2. John H. Jenkins, *Basic Texas Books, An Annotated Bibliography of Selected Works for a Research Library,* rev. ed. (Austin: Texas State Historical Association, 1988), pp. 373–79.

3. Ibid., p. 377.

4. Jenkins points out the error in *Basic Texas Books,* p. 377.

5. *Travels and Adventures in Texas in the 1820's: Being the Reminiscences of Mary Crownover Rabb* (Waco, Tex.: W. M. Morrison, 1962); Teresa Vielé, *"Following the Drum": A Glimpse of Frontier Life* (1858; reprint, Lincoln: University of Nebraska Press, 1984).

6. There are several editions of the Matthews book. The most recent

and best is the Texas A & M University Press edition of 1982 with illustrations by noted Texas artists E. M (Buck) Schiwetz and a companion volume by Frances Mayhugh Holden, *Lambshead Before Interwoven* (1982). For further information, see Jenkins, *Basic Texas Books,* pp. 373–75.

7. Rabb and her husband were among the early Austin colonists. As far as we know, hers is the only woman's diary to survive from this important period of Texas history.

8. For a brief sketch of Samuel Maverick's life, see Walter Prescott Webb and H. Bailey Carroll, eds., *The Handbook of Texas,* 2 vols. (Austin: Texas State Historical Association, 1952), 2:161. There will undoubtedly be a longer and more complete entry in the new revised *Handbook,* but it is not scheduled for publication until 1990. In the meantime, those interested in both Samuel and Mary Ann Maverick should read the excellent biography by Paula Marks, "Turn Your Eyes toward Bexar: Sam and Mary Maverick on the Texas Frontier" (Ph.D. diss., University of Texas at Austin, 1987). It is currently in press at Texas A & M University Press, College Station, Texas.

9. Elizabeth B. Custer, *Tenting on the Plains; or, General Custer in Kansas and Texas* (1887; reprint, 3 vols. with an introduction by Jane K. Stewart, Norman: University of Oklahoma Press, 1971).

10. Rabb, *Adventures and Travels,* pp. 8–9.

11. Maverick's diaries are in the Maverick papers, Barker Texas History Center, University of Texas at Austin. See also Marks, "Turn Your Eyes toward Bexar." On Mary's interest in spiritualism, see p. 101, and on her use of homeopathic medicine see especially pp. 94 and 104–5.

12. On the Tonkawas and Karankawas, see W. W. Newcomb, Jr., *The Indians of Texas: From Prehistoric to Modern Times* (1961; reprint, Austin: University of Texas Press, in cooperation with the Texas State Historical Association, 1969).

13. Webb and Carroll, *Handbook of Texas,* 2: 424. As they note, this fight was "probably the greatest blunder in the history of Texas Indian relations . . . and prolonged the war with the Comanche . . . and made future, orderly, friendly contact between the government and the Comanche almost impossible."

14. Ibid., 2:161.

15. On this point, see especially Jenkins, *Basic Texas Books,* pp. 378–79.

16. For the details of Mary Maverick's later life, I am indebted to Paula Marks, "Turn Your Eyes toward Bexar" and her entry for the forthcoming revised *Handbook of Texas.*

PREFACE.

This little book is written for my children—they have often requested me to put into shape the notes and memoranda which I have jotted down during the early days. I have based the following history of my family, and of events transpiring near us, upon my own, and upon some of Mr. Maverick's notes, which were made at the time. I have drawn somewhat from family tradition, from letters written contemporaneously, occasionally from books of authority for dates, and I have not failed to consult with many of the survivors of those early days. I have in some instances relied on my memory, but not often. I trust it will be of use in cementing my descendants together in the distant future, as they are now united in the spirit of kindly kinship. I am so impressed with the idea that the work will be useful in the influence indicated, and that my allotted time on earth is drawing toward its ending, that in my old days I have roused myself up, have experienced again the joys and the sorrows of those dear old times, and now, my dear children, the work is finished. Jesus said: "I must work the work of Him that sent me, while it is day; the night cometh, when no man can work."

MARY A. MAVERICK.

San Antonio, Texas, March, 1881.

Chapter I.

FAMILY HISTORY—ANCESTORS.

MY maiden name was Mary Ann Adams. I was born March 16th, 1818, in Tuskaloosa County, Alabama. My parents were William Lewis Adams, of Lynchburg, and his wife Agatha Strother Lewis, of Botetourt County,* both of the state of Virginia.

My father was son of Robert Adams, from Massachusetts, and his wife Mary Lynch, of Lynchburg, Virginia. John Lynch, brother of Mary Lynch, was one of the leading men of Lynchburg.

My mother was a member of an extensive and well known family in Virginia. John Lewis, the founder of the Lewis family in America, married Margaret Lynn, daughter of the Laird of Loch Lynn, Scotland. General Andrew Lewis was the second son of the union. He was a prominent man in Colonial days, and a particular friend of Washington.* His wife was Elizabeth Givens. He commanded the Colonial forces at the great Indian battle of Point Pleasant, where the savages were totally overthrown, and where his younger brother, Colonel Charles Lewis, distinguished for gallantry, was killed. Upon the suggestion of General Washington, General Andrew Lewis was appointed a Brigadier General in the American Army, on the breaking out of the Revolutionary war. He was then prematurely old, and died in 1780, having passed his sixty-second year. His statue was placed in the well known group, by the Sculptor Crawford, in the Capitol Grounds at Richmond, Virginia, where my son George Madison and I saw it in 1876·

---

*Now Roanoke County.

*See Theodore Roosevelt's, The Winning of the West, Vol. 1, Chapters VII, VIII, IX.

William Lewis, of Fincastle, Botetourt County, Virginia, my grandfather, was the youngest son of General Andrew Lewis. He married Lucy Madison. in Washington County, Virginia, in 1788. Lucy Madison's parents were John Madison and Agatha Strother Madison. John Madison was first cousin of James Madison, President of the United States. A son of John Madison, James Madison, was President of William and Mary College, and Bishop of Virginia. Another son, George Madison, married a sister of Chief Justice Marshall of the United States Supreme Court and became afterwards Governor of Kentucky. John Madison had another son, Rollin, and several daughters, one of whom was Lucy, as above stated. From this marriage of John Lewis and Lucy Madison were born two children, Agatha Strother, my mother, and Andrew. My grandmother died in 1792, and by a second marriage, with Ann McClanahan, my grandfather had other children.

Samuel Augustus Maverick, my husband, was born July 23rd, 1803, at Pendleton, South Carolina. His parents were Samuel Maverick and his wife Elizabeth Anderson. She was the daughter of General Robert Anderson, of South Carolina, and of Revolutionary note, and his wife Ann Thompson of Virginia. Samuel Maverick was once a prominent merchant of Charleston, S. C., where he had raised himself from the almost abject poverty, to which the war of the Revolution had reduced his family, to a position of great affluence. It is said of him that he sent ventures to the Celestial Empire, and that he shipped the first bale of cotton from America to Europe. Some mercantile miscarriage caused him subsequently to withdraw from, and close out, his business, and he retired to Pendleton District* in the north west corner of South Carolina, at the foot of the mountains. Here he spent the balance of his days, and invested and speculated largely in lands in South Carolina, Georgia and Alabama.

The Mavericks entered America at three prominent points—Boston, New York and Charleston, South Caro-

---

*Now· Oconee County.

lina. It seems the New York family came during the American Revolution, and were not related to the others. The Mavericks of Boston and Charleston were probably closely related, at any rate they must have been of the same family in England. Samuel is a family name with them—the Boston family had many Samuels, as also the Charleston family. A Samuel Maverick was shot by the British, in the Boston massacre March 5th, 1770*. Much of the history of the Boston Mavericks is to be found in a book entitled "History of East Boston" by William H. Sumner, published 1858. In that book is the following statement: "With the destruction of the town records, at the burning of Charlestown on June 17th, 1775, were lost the only means of making a full genealogical account" of the Maverick family.

The Charleston, South Carolina, branch of the family preserved no regular records—some few facts and some traditions are all we have left. Samuel Maverick, father of my husband displayed a coat of arms, and he occasionally spoke of an ancestor, Margaret Coyer, who was a Huguenot, banished from France, and from whom he inherited the privilege. He called his place in Pendleton, Montpelier, for her ancestral home in Southern France. I have no doubt Samuel Maverick had many old family papers and memoranda in his house, which were destroyed when the house burned down in 184.....

Many incidents in my husband's life I do not allude to in this book, for they are mentioned in the "Eulogy on the Life and Character of Honorable Samuel A. Maverick" delivered October 1870, before the Alamo Literary Society of San Antonio, Texas, by George Cupples, M. D.

---

*The Commonwealth of Massachusetts erected a monument which stands on Boston Common to the memory of the four men killed in the "Boston Massacre," one of whom was the youth, Samuel Maverick.

Chapter II.

EARLY MARRIED DAYS.

ON Thursday, August 4th, A. D., 1836, at my widowed mother's home and plantation, three miles north of Tuskaloosa, Alabama, I was married to Samuel A. Maverick, of the Republic of Texas, formerly of Pendleton, South Carolina, Reverend Mathews, of Christ's Episcopal Church officiating. On the 8th, we left for a visit to Shelby Springs of one month, thence to Talladega Springs, and a few days visit to Judge Shortridge's. Here we met his daughter, my classmate and intimate friend, Mrs. E. A. Lewis, wife of Dr. Hamilton Lewis of Mobile. Maggie Shortridge, sister of Mrs. Lewis, soon after married Dr. Philip Pearson of South Carolina, and they moved to Victoria, Texas, and thence settled on Caney, near the Hardemans.

From Talladega we went to Florence and Tuscumbia, and visited on the plantation six miles from Florence, Mrs. Joseph Thompson, sister of Mr. Maverick. We spent three or four days there, and one day with my aunt, Mrs. John Bradley, also one day with Uncle John Lewis, returning to mother's in October. January 1837 we went to Mobile and New Orleans, and rode eight miles on the railroad from Lake Pontchartrain to the City of New Orleans—the first railroad I ever saw, and the first built in the south. We returned to mother's on February 28th.

On March 12th, 1837, we left mother's again, this time in our own carriage, to visit Father Maverick in South Carolina. We arrived at "Montpelier," Father's place on 19th, and had a most joyful reception. Father had not seen his only son "Gus," for such was he called by his relatives, and by the colored people, "Mars Gus,"—for

STORMING OF THE ALAMO, FROM PAINTING BY T. GENTILZ

several years. He had in fact, at one time, counted and mourned him as lost in the "fall of the Alamo" in Texas. We were treated with the greatest affection. Father fondly hoped to induce his son to settle there. He offered to give him "Montpelier"—mills, vineyards, orchards, lands, and shops—if he would accept them—or another place,

"Gibbs," a new style house and improvements: but all in vain, for my husband dreamed constantly of Texas, and said: "We must go back."

Poor father looked sad and afflicted at the mention of our going, and so we said very little about it, and agreed to stay as long as Mr. Maverick could.

Here, on Sunday, May 14th, 1837, was born our son Sam.

We spent a pleasant summer with father, who was very fond of us all, and especially of baby. Father had three children living at this time—my husband, his only son, and two daughters, Elizabeth and Lydia. Elizabeth married Mr. Joseph Weyman and had three children by that marriage—Elizabeth, now Mrs. Dr. G. J. Houston, living in San Antonio, Texas, Joseph B. and Augustus. Her husband died and she married Mr. Thompson, from which union were born Samuel and Josephine, now Mrs. Hardin, of Memphis, Tennessee.

His other daughter Lydia married Mr. William Van-Wyck, of New York City.

But, notwithstanding the endearments held out to us by Father, my husband adhered, without flinching, to his purpose of uniting his destiny with Texas. At last he set the time for departure and made every preparation for a great journey by land to the new El Dorado.

Chapter III.
HO, FOR THE LONE STAR!

ON the 14th day of October 1837, baby five months old, we bade goodbye to "Montpelier" and the servants and set off for Texas. Father accompanied us half a day, and it was a sad sight to witness his grief when he at last parted with his son. My heart ached for the dear old man. We travelled in a carriage, Mr. Maverick driving and nurse Rachel and baby and myself the other occupants. In a wagon with Wiley as driver was Jinny, our cook to be, and her four children. Reached Mother's about the last of October, and stopped with her about six weeks, making final preparations. Mother consented to let my youngest brother Robert go to Texas with us—he was fifteen, but slight and pale, having been quite sick during the fall. My brother William was already in Texas.

December 7th, 1837, we set off for Texas. With heavy hearts we said goodbye to Mother, and my brothers and sister. Mother ran after us for one more embrace. She held me in her arms and wept aloud, and said: "Oh, Mary, I will never see you again on Earth." I felt heartbroken and often recalled that thrilling cry; and I have never beheld my dear Mother again.

Our party was composed of four whites, counting baby, and ten negroes. The negroes were four men, Griffin, Granville, Wiley and Uncle Jim—two women, Jinny and Rachael, and Jinny's four children, Jack, Betsy, Lavinia and Jane. Uncle Jim was Robert's man, Griffin, Granville and Rachael belonged to me, a gift from my Mother, and the others were Mr. Maverick's individual property. We had a large carriage, a big Kentucky wagon, three extra saddle horses and one blooded filly. The wagon carried a tent, a supply of provisions and bedding, and the cook and children. We had a delightful trip all through, with the exception of four days' journey across a prairie swamp and one night's adventure with Indians, which I will mention in their order. We occasionally stopped several days in a good place, to rest, to have washing done, and sometimes to give muddy roads time to dry, and we had no serious trouble or accident throughout. We crossed the Mississippi at Rodney, and Red River at Alexandria, and came through bottoms in Louisiana where the high-water marks on the trees stood far above our carriage top, but the roads were good then. We crossed the Sabine, a sluggish, muddy, narrow stream, and stood upon the soil of the Republic of Texas,* about New Years day, 1838.

1838.

January 7th, 1838, we occupied an empty cabin in San Augustine, while the carriage was being repaired. This was a poor little village, principally of log cabins on one street, but the location was high and dry. We laid in a supply of corn and groceries here and pushed on through Nacogdoches to the Place of Col. Durst, an old acquaintance of Mr. Maverick's. Mrs. Durst was a Virginia lady and a fine housekeeper—we spent a day or two there. There we met General Rusk,* also an old friend of Mr. Maverick's and formerly of Pendleton, S. C.

We now had to travel in occasional rains and much mud, where the country was poor and sparsely settled and provisions for man and beast scarce. On advice we selected the longest, but the best road, namely the road leading via Washington, high up on the Brazos. From

---

*Las Tekas: Name of the home village of the Nassonite Indians, on the East bank of the Neches River.

The Frenchman La Harpe claims the Province of Las Tekas as part of Louisiana in 1719, in contending with the Spanish Governor D'Alarconne.

*Thomas J. Rusk was of Irish descent, a brave soldier, lawyer and statesman. He came to Texas in 1834—signed the Declaration of Texas Independence, was the friend and advisor of Sam Houston and fought gallantly at San Jacinto; in this battle Colonel Almonte surrendered to Colonel Rusk.

Rusk filled many public offices and was elected United States Senator by Texas' first Legislature.

Washington we went to Columbus, on the Colorado, and thence about due south towards the Lavaca River.

Now came a dreadful time; about January 26th, we entered a bleak, desolate, swamp-prairie, cut up by what were called "dry bayous," i. e. deep gullies, and now almost full of water. This swamp, crossed by the "Sandy," "Mustang" and the head branches of the Navidad, was fourteen miles wide. We had passed Mr. Bridge's, the last house before we got into this dreadful prairie, and had to cross the Navidad before we got to Mr. Keer's, the next habitation. Every step of the animals was in water, sometimes knee-deep. We stalled in five or six gullies, and each time the wagon had to be unloaded in water, rain and north wind and all the men and animals had to work together to pull out.

The first Norther I ever experienced struck us here—this norther was a terrific howling north wind with a fine rain, blowing and penetrating through clothes and blankets—never in my life had I felt such cold. We were four days crossing this dreadful fourteen miles of swamp. The first day we made three miles and that night my mattress floated in water which fell in extra quantities during the night. The baby and I were tolerably dry; all the others were almost constantly wet during the four weary monotonous days—but no one suffered any bad effects from the great exposure, and Mr. Maverick kept cheerful all the while and was not a bit discouraged that we could see—said that water was better than mud to pull in and that we were only eight or nine miles from Keer's. Our corn had given out and our provisions were about gone when, on the 30th, we reached the Navidad. The men "hollooed" at a great rate and, after long continued calling men appeared on the opposite bank. Soon we were ferried over, and were all warmed, comforted, fed and treated like kinfolk. Mrs. Keer and Miss Sue Linn were ever so nice to us.

February 4th, we reached "Spring Hill," Major Sutherland's on the Navidad, where we all, except Mr. Maver-

ick, remained until 2nd of June. Mr. Maverick went on
to see whether it was safe to take us to San Antonio. He
also visited Cox's point on Matagorda Bay, opposite Lavaca, with a view of possibly locating there. There he
owned land, but he decided in favor of San Antonio. In
February, at Sutherland's, two of our horses froze to
death in a norther. April 18th, Mr. Maverick went to
New Orleans to purchase furniture, clothing, provisions,
etc., for beginning housekeeping, and returned to us in
May.

At Spring Hill, boarded Mrs. Roylston, a young widow
with her son,—also Captain Sylvester, from Ohio, who
had captured Santa Anna after the battle of San Jacinto,*
and Captain Peck of the Louisiana Greys,* who was
engaged to be married to a niece of Mrs. Sutherland,
Miss Fannie Menifee, who lived beyond the Navidad and
was the belle of Jackson County. Fannie and I attended
a San Jacinto ball at Texana, on April 21st. Her brother John Menifee, one of the heroes of that battle, escorted
us, and there was quite a gathering. Miss Fannie received
great attention. In April, Major Sutherland's corn gave
out, and he went over to Egypt for a supply. Egypt is on
the Colorado, near Eagle Lake. We called Mrs. Sutherland "Aunt Fannie"—her eldest son William, a young
man of nineteen, just home from school, went to San Antonio to learn Spanish, and was killed with Travis at the
"Fall of the Alamo"* March 6th, 1836. I learned from

*See Gen. Houston's official report of San Jacinto battle. Thrall's His. P. 265.
  *Two companies fitted out by the citizens of New Orleans to help the
Texans' cause.
  *The Alamo or Church of the Mission of the Alamo, "Alamo" being Spanish for
cottonwood tree, was formerly surrounded by cottonwoods. The corner stone
was laid 1744. It was also called Mission San Antonio de Velero, because it
was removed by order of the Viceroy of New Spain, the Marquis de Velero, May
1st, 1718, from the banks of the Rio Grande.
  "The famous siege began February 22nd, 1836. The 'Fall of the Alamo' took
place March 6, 1836." One hundred and seventy Texans with such courageous
leaders as Travis, Bowie, "Davy" Crockett and Bonham determined never to
surrender or retreat to Santa Anna's overwhelming forces, (some 4000), and all
were killed.
  Kendall writing in 1841 says, "The Alamo is now in ruins," and so it remained for thirteen years or so after "the fall." In about 1849 Major Babbitt,
U. S. A., made use of it as a Quartermaster's Depot and in order to do this had
almost to rebuild it. "Deep down in the debris were found two or three skeletons
that had evidently been hastily covered with rubbish after the 'fall,' for with
them were found fur caps and buckskin trappings, undoubted relics of the ever
memorable last stand." See Wm. Corner in San Antonio de Bexar, p. 11.

her and the other ladies many thrilling tales of the run-
away times of '36—when women and children fled in
terror before the advancing forces under Santa Anna—
savages who burnt and plundered and committed all
kinds of outrages. They told me it rained almost every
day for six weeks of that dreadful time.

One day, Old "Bowls," Cherokee chief, with twelve or
thirteen of his tribe, coming from Houston, camped at
Spring Hill, near the house. After tea, we were dancing,
when "Bowls" came in dressed in a breech-cloth, anklets,
moccasins, feathers and a long, clean, white linen shirt,
which had been presented to him in Houston. He said the
pretty ladies in Houston had danced with, kissed him and
given him rings. We, however, begged to be excused
and requested him to retire, when he in great contempt
stalked out, and our dance broke up. Bowls told us President Houston had lived in his Nation, that he had given
Houston his daughter for his squaw and had made him
a "big chief;" but that now he was no longer Cherokee,
but "The Great Father" of the white men.

On Saturday, June 2nd we set off from "Spring Hill"
for San Antonio de Bexar, in those days frequently called
simply "Bexar,"* which is now the name of the county
only. Ten miles to Texana and three miles to Dry Branch
—on 3rd, 12 miles to Natches and three miles to De Leon's
rancho, on the Garcitas—on the 4th, six miles to Casa
Blanca and nine miles to Victoria, a village on the Guadalupe. On the 5th, eight miles to Arroyo Coleto—6th,
twelve miles to Arroyo Manahuilla, where a wagon
wheel broke, and Mr. Maverick went to Goliad to
have it mended, but failing, we mended it as well as we
could with rawhide* and false spokes.

It was two or three miles north of the main road and
east of the Manahuilla, on Easter Sunday, March 27th,
1836, that Col. Fannin was surprised by the Mexican General Urrea. Urrea surrounded Fannin's forces with a

---

*The name San Antonio de Bexar seems to have been used only in connection
with the presidio or military post of San Antonio about 1733 in contrast to the
village of San Antonio de Velero. See S. A. de Bexar, Wm. Corner.

*Texas cowboys used to say ''Texas is bound together with rawhide.''

largely superior force, (lately victors of the "Alamo" and Travis) and, then offering honorable terms of capitulation he induced Fannin, thinking to spare bloodshed, to surrender as prisoners of war his whole force, consisting of four hundred and eighty men in all. They were marched to Goliad, and the next morning were formed into line and shot down in cold blood. Santa Anna had so ordered —Urrea refused to perform the bloody deed, but Colonel Gavrie, infamous name be it forever! executed the order. Fifty-five escaped. On June 3d, 1836, General Thomas J. Rusk collected and buried the bones, which had been left bleaching on the plain after the bodies had been burnt. Gen. Rusk delivered a moving address over the ashes, bones and charred human flesh; and "there was not a dry eye in the soldier ranks."

June 7th, we travelled five miles to Goliad, on the left bank of the San Antonio River, and camped in the old mission of La Bahia.

Chapter IV.

TONKAWA INDIANS.

ON June 8th, we went eighteen miles to Ojo de Agua, and nine miles to Harris's on the Ecleto. On the 9th, we went nine miles from Harris's place and our wagon broke down. Mr. Maverick was hunt_ ing in the San Antonio River bottom for wood to mend the wheel, when he met Mr. Harris, who, being a wheelright, agreed to mend the wheel if we would take it back to his place. Some of our people were sick, and Robert, Griffin and Jinnie had chills every second day, so we left the main party tented and went back with the wheel to Harris's. He was very kind, but had very poor accommodations and his cabin swarmed with fleas. He had two very nice little daughters. Some weeks later, while the girls were off visiting relatives, the Indians killed Mr. Harris, burnt his home and took off his horses.

June 12th, late in the afternoon, we reached camp again, and were loading up to move on two or three miles further to a better camping place for the night, when several Indians rode up. They said "Mucho Amigo," (dear friend) and were loud and filthy and manifested their intention to be very intimate. More and more came until we counted seventeen! They rode in amongst us, looked constantly at the horses, and it is no exaggeration to say, they annoyed us very much. They were Tonkawas, said they were just from a battle, in which they were victors, on the Nueces River, where they had fought the Comanches two days before. They were in war paint, and well armed, and displayed in triumph two scalps, one hand, and several pieces of putrid flesh from various parts of the human body. These were to be taken

New-Haven A.D. 1823

S. A. Maverick Left Charleston South-Carolina
and sailed for New-York —— 30 May 1822
Remained in N. York 2 weeks from thence went to
New Haven, Thence to Ripton 14 miles where I
remained studying under Mr Rudd until Commencem.t
Entered Yale Col at commencement —— Sept 1822
Sophomore Class which I entered contains 105 Students.
Total Undergraduates 373. Presd. Jeremiah Day.
September Vacation, traveled up the Connecticut
via Hartford, Middletown, Springfield, Northampton &c.
Term of Study from last of Oct till 2 wednesday Jany
Went to New-York (city) —— Jan 7. 1823
Term of Study from Jany 'till May
May vacation go to Norwalk, Stratford &c ——
Dear Father and sisters are in New York from
Charleston + went to new york + came to N. Haven
with them ab.t 1.st June. —— May. 1823..
Term commences ——
Third Term of Sophomore: hardest studies. Spherics &c!
Commenced this Book this day —— 10 June 1823

to the squaws to eat and dance around when
these warriors rejoined the tribe. I was frightened
almost to death, but tried not to show my alarm. They
rode up to the carriage window and asked to see the
"papoose." First one, then another came, and I held up
my little Sammy, and smiled at their complaints. But I
took care to have my pistol and bowie knife visible, and
kept cool, and declined most decidedly when they asked
me to hand the baby out to them that they might "see
how pretty and white" he was. I knew, and so did we all,
though we did not tell each other till afterwards, that
they, being cannibals, would like to eat my baby, and kill
us all and carry off our horses. But we had six men fully
armed and determined and all hands kept steadily loading
the wagons, saddling the horses and preparing to move. I
kept telling Griffin to hurry the others, and Mr. Maverick
worked coolly with the rest. Jinny said "Let's cook some
supper first," and grumbled mightily when Griffin ordered her into the wagon and drove off. Imagine our con-
sternation when the Indians turned back, and every one
of the seventeen rode along with us! It was a bright moon-
light night, and Griffin and one other on horseback acted
as our rear guard. About midnight, some of the Indians,
finding we were so unsociable and seeing that we were
dangerous, commenced dropping behind, and one by one
they turned back, until at early dawn, when we reached
the Cibolo, having travelled eighteen miles during the
night, only two Indians were still attendant. Here we
camped and the two Indians sat down, not far off, in an
observant attitude. I went into my tent to lie down, and
Griffin said "Don't be afraid, Miss Mary, but go to sleep,"
and I saw him sit down in front of the tent, with his gun,
and an ax in his hands which he shook at the Indians, and
said: "Come this way if you dare, you devils, and I'll
make hash out of you!" I went to sleep with the baby and
when I waked, all the vile Indians were gone, everybody
rested, and my breakfast and dinner were both waiting
for me. That certainly was a narrow escape from a

cruel death.   The Tonkawas were treacherous and cruel and noted thieves and murderers.

It was well we did not trust them. I will give an opposite illustration of Indian treachery in an event which happened only about two weeks after this experience of ours. On June 27th, or 28th, 1838, whilst a party consisting of a surveyor, chain bearers and others was surveying on the Rio Frio, a party of Comanche Indians came to their camp saying "Mucho Amigo," and asking for food. They were welcomed and sat down with the whites, and whilst all were eating together, the Indians sprang up suddenly, killed the surveyor, wounded another man and stampeded and stole every one of their horses.

Chapter V.

SAN ANTONIO DE BEXAR.

E were now travelling up the valley of the San Antonio River, occasionally passing along the left bank of the river itself. June 13, sixteen miles to the Marcelino Creek and three miles to Aroche's rancho near Erasmo Seguin's—14th, eight miles to Jesus Cantu's ranch'o on the arroyo Calaveras, passing several other ranchos, eleven miles to the Salado. June 15th, 1838 nine miles to "El Presidio de San Antonio de Bexar." Senor Don Jose Casiano, whose rancho we passed, had offered us his city house until we had time to secure another. This polite offer we accepted and immediately occupied Mr. Casiano's house, when we entered the town. This place fronted on the Main Plaza (Plaza Major), was bounded south by Dolorosa Street and extended half way back to the Military Plaza. It is now covered by the east half of the Hord Hotel.*

The front room of the house was then occupied by my brother William Adams as a store. He was so much afflicted with the "Texas fever" that soon after my wedding he set out for San Antonio, travelling on horseback from Galveston. Before reaching San Antonio, he dreamt several times of the town and its surroundings, and when he reached the hills east of town he was struck with the faithful resemblance between the reality and his dreams. He looked upon it as something marvelous and frequently spoke of his prophetic dreams. He was twenty-two then, and he immediately determined to establish himself as a merchant in San Antonio. He bought a horse

---

*At present, Southern Hotel.

which he named Mexico or "Mex" and rode him all the way back to Tuskaloosa. William turned all his available property in Tuskaloosa into money, bought goods, brought them to San Antonio, rented the room of Casiano, and set up as a merchant. He rode back on the horse "Mex," which horse by the way, Mr. Maverick afterwards bought, and we used "Mex" in the "run-away" of '42 and when we removed from La Grange to the Peninsula in 1844, Mr. Maverick, after our arrival, put in some money with William. Dr. Launcelot Smithers was William's clerk and success seemed certain, but Smithers sold large amounts on credit to Mexicans in Coahuila; and, though the Mexicans were well to do, they never paid, and after eighteen months merchandizing William closed up without realizing the capital invested. William left February 1st, 1839, for Mother's to bring out his negros and try farming. He returned with brother Andrew October, 1839.

We lived in the Casiano house until about September 1st, when we moved into a house north of, and adjoining, the historic Veramendi place. The house we rented belonged to the Huisars. Huisar, the ancestor, carved the beautiful doors for the San Jose Mission—he had quite a number of workmen under him and was employed several years in the work. In the latter part of December, Mr. Maverick went to Mobile to get some money in the hands of John Aiken, his attorney. Aiken was then in Tuskaloosa, where, as Mr. Maverick's agent, he had sold to a Mr. Brown for sixteen thousand dollars Mr. Maverick's business stores in that place. Part of the money was paid down and Mr. Maverick returned to us in January.

1839.

Early in February, 1839, we had a heavy snow storm, the snow drifted in some places to a depth of two feet, and on the north side of our house it lasted five or six days. Anton Lockmar rigged up a sleigh and took some girls riding up and down Soledad Street. Early in February, we moved into our own house, at the north east corner of Commerce and Soledad Streets, being also the north east corner of the Main Plaza, (Plaza Mayor.) This house remained our homestead until July '49, over ten years, although five of the ten years,—from '42 to '47, we wandered about as refugees. It was known as the Barrera place, when Mr. Maverick purchased it, and the deed dated January 19th, 1839.

The main house was of stone, and had three rooms, one fronting south on Main Street and west on Soledad Street and the other two fronting west on Soledad Street—also a shed in the yard along the east wall of the house towards the north end. This shed we closed in with an adobe* wall and divided into a kitchen and servant's room. We also built an adobe servant's room on Soledad Street, leaving a gateway between it and the main house, and we built a stable near the river.

We built a strong but homely picket fence around the garden to the north and fenced the garden off from the yard. In the garden were sixteen large fig trees and many rows of old pomegranates. In the yard were several China trees, and on the river bank just below our line in the De la Zerda premises was a grand old cypress, which we could touch through our fence, and its roots made ridges in our yard. The magnificent old tree stands there today. It made a great shade and we erected our bath house and wash place under its spreading branches.

Our neighbors on the east, Main or Commerce Street, were the De la Zerdas. In 1840, their place was leased to a Greek, Roque Catahdie, who kept a shop on the street and lived in the back rooms. He married a pretty, bright-eyed Mexican girl of fourteen years, dressed her in jewelry and fine clothes and bought her a dilapidated piano— he was jealous and wished her to amuse herself at home. The piano had the desired effect, and she enjoyed it like a child with a new trinket. The fame of her piano went through the town, and, after tea, crowds would come to

---

*Sun dried bricks, often in San Antonio, soft stone, usually plastered on the outside to protect from the weather.

witness her performance. One night Mrs. Elliott and I took a peep and we found a large crowd inside laughing and applauding, and other envious ones gazing in from the street.

Our neighbor on the north, Soledad Street, was Dona Juana Varcinez, and I must not omit her son Leonicio. She had cows and sold me the strippings of the milk at twenty-five cents per gallon, and we made our butter from this. Mrs. McMullen was the only person then who made butter for sale, and her butter was not good, although she received half a dollar per pound for it. Old Juana was a kind old soul—had the earliest pumpkins, a great delicacy, at twenty-five cents and spring chickens at twelve and a half cents. She opened up the spring gardening by scratching with a dull hoe, some holes in which she planted pumpkin seed—then later she planted corn, red pepper, garlic, onions, etc. She was continually calling to Leonicio to drive the chickens out of the garden, or bring in the dogs from the street. She told me this answered two purposes—it kept Leonicio at home out of harm's way, and gave him something to do. She had lots of dogs—one fat, lazy pelon (hairless dog) slept with the old lady to keep her feet warm. When we returned from the coast in '47, Sam S. Smith had purchased the place from her and he was living there. He was a good and kind neighbor.

We moved into our home in good time, for here on Sunday morning, March 23d, 1839, was born our second child, Lewis Antonio. All my friends have always told me, and, until quite recently I was persuaded Lewis was the first child of pure American stock born in San Antonio.* But now I understand a Mr. Brown with his wife came here in 1828 for two years from East Texas, and during that time a son was born to them in San Antonio. Mr. Brown, the father, died about the same time of consumption, and his wife moved away further East. The son named John Brown, is now said to be a citizen of Waco,

---

*Lewis Antonio Maverick, however, was the first child born in San Antonio of American parents to ''grow up'' in San Antonio and Mary A. Maverick the first American born woman or United States woman to make San Antonio her home.

During the summer, Sammy had difficulty teething. Dr. Weideman, a Russian scholar and naturalist, and an excellent physician and surgeon, took a great liking to Sammy and prescribed for him with success. This summer, William B. Jacques brought his wife and two little girls, and settled on Commerce Street. In the latter part of August, Mr. William Elliott brought his wife and two children, Mary and Billy, to San Antonio. They bought a house on the west side of Soledad Street, opposite the north end of our garden, and we were a great many years neighbors and always friends. This year our negro men plowed and planted one labor* above the Alamo and were attacked by Indians. Griffin and Wiley ran into the river and saved themselves. The Indians cut the traces and took off the work animals and we did not farm there again. Mr. Thomas Higginbotham, a carpenter, with his wife, came to San Antonio and took the house opposite us on the corner of Commerce Street and Main Plaza. His brother and sister settled in the country, on the river below San José Mission. This year the town of Seguin on the Guadalupe thirty-five miles east of San Antonio, was founded.

In November, 1839, a party of ladies and gentlemen from Houston came to visit San Antonio—they rode on horseback. The ladies were Miss Trask of Boston, Mass., and Miss Evans, daughter of Judge Evans of Texas. The gentlemen were Judge Evans, and Colonel J. W. Dancey, Secretary of War, Republic of Texas. They were, ladies and all, armed with pistols and bowie knifes. I rode with this party and some others around the head of the San Antonio river. We galloped up the west side, and paused at and above the head of the river long enough to view and admire the lovely valley of the San Antonio. The leaves had mostly fallen from the trees, and left the view open to the Missions below. The day was clear, cool and bright, and we saw three of the missions, including San Juan Capistrano seven miles below town. We

*Labor: Spanish land measure of about 177 acres.

galloped home, down the east side, and doubted not that Indians watched us from the heavy timber of the river bottom.   The gentlemen of the party numbered six, and we were all mounted on fine animals.

SAN FERNANDO CATHEDRAL, MAIN PLAZA
(Present Front Added 1873)

MISSION CONCEPCION (First Mission)

Chapter VI.

COMANCHES.

The experiences of my first years in Texas led me to think the Comanches were an active and vigorous tribe of Indians. At that time they were about the only Indians who infested the country in the vicinity of San Antonio, and I must mention here some of their deeds which held our attention at the time.

June 29th, 1838, thirty-eight Comanches came into the edge of town and killed two Mexicans and stole one boy—on the 30th they killed a German and a Mexican. July 1st, the flag of Texas waves on the Plaza in front of the Court House, and a company of volunteers are assembling for pursuit of the Indians. Later, our company of volunteers fell in with a considerable party of Comanches, attacked them, killed two and wounded many others—but the wounded were carried off by the others, all of whom beat a hasty retreat. Our people captured all their horses and provisions.

The Mexicans of Mexico have not forgotten us. About this time, a party of Mexicans, 200 strong under Agaton, learning that valuable goods had been landed at Capano, and were being carted by friendly Mexicans to the San Antonio merchants, crossed the Rio Grande at Matamoras, captured the train and compelled the cartmen to haul the goods to the Nueces river where the cartmen were dismissed. Of the two Americans who were with the train when it was captured, one was killed and the other was wounded, but escaped.

During July, 1838 many rumors from the west came to the effect that an army of centralists was marching to capture Bexar—also that the Comanche Nation had entered into a treaty of alliance with the Mexicans and would act with them for our extermination. But in a day or two, it was ascertained that Aristo had pursued the "President of the Republic of the Rio Grande," General Vidauria, who having been defeated in battle had fled to Texas for refuge. Aristo turned back at the Nueces.

But I have promised to speak of the Indians. In the stable we built on our home lot, Mr. Maverick kept a fine blooded horse, fastened by a heavy pad-locked chain to a mesquite-picket. The door of the stable was securely locked also, for every precaution was necessary to prevent his being stolen. This was the "war horse." Mr. Maverick was a member of the Volunteer Company of "Minute Men" commanded by the celebrated Jack Hays* —who is now an honored citizen of California. Each volunteer kept a good horse, saddle, bridle and arms, and a supply of coffee, salt, sugar and other provisions ready at any time to start on fifteen minutes warning, in pursuit of marauding Indians. At a certain signal given by the Cathedral bell, the men were off, in buckskin clothes and blankets responding promptly to the call. They were organized to follow the Indians to their mountain fastnesses and destroy their villages, if they failed to kill the Indians.

---

*John Coffee Hays or "Jack" Hays was born January 28, 1817 at Little Cedar Lick, Wilson County, Tenn., close to the "Hermitage," which was originally a part of the Hays property.

His father and grandfather distinguished themselves in Creek wars under Jackson. Hays left home at the age of fifteen to survey land in Mississippi. At the age of nineteen he joined the Texan Army at Brazos River just after San Jacinto battle. Besides leading the "Minute Men" in San Antonio he commanded in numerous battles against Mexico, and was commissioned by the Texas Congress, in 1840, first Captain of the Texas Rangers. He distinguished himself repeatedly in the Mexican war and later crossed the plains to California in '49 where he filled courageously many positions of public trust. He died in Piedmont, California, April 28, 1883. John Hays Hammond was a nephew.

Hittell's History of California gives the following incident in connection with Hays' election as first sheriff of San Francisco—it seems his opponent was a saloonkeeper who represented the lawless element of the town; on the day of election the latter opened to the public free of charge his choicest liquors, to curry favor and secure votes. Wishing to hear how the election was going, on the afternoon of the election day, Hays rode into the public square on his splendid mettlesome steed, whereupon the crowd, carried away by his noble appearance, cheered wildly and elected him forthwith.

Some buildings and the original fence of Hays' San Antonio home still stand on N. W. cor. of Presa and Nueva Sts., San Antonio.

Jack Hays came from Tennessee to Texas just after the battle of San Jacinto and when he came to San Antonio he was nineteen years of age, at which time he was appointed a deputy surveyor. The surveying parties frequently had "brushes" with the Indians, and it was on these occasions that Hays displayed such rare military skill and daring, that very soon by consent of all, he was looked upon as the leader and his orders were obeyed and he himself loved by all. In a fight he was utterly fearless and invincible.

There were many remarkable young men in San Antonio at that time who were attracted by the climate by the novelty, or by the all-absorbing spirit of land speculation. They volunteered from almost every state of the Union to come and fight in the short but bloody struggle of '35 and '36 for the freedom of Texas. Many came too late, i. e., after San Jacinto, but were drawn to the west by the wildness and danger and daring of the frontier life. They were a noble and gallant set or "boys" as they styled each other and soon the Indians grew less aggressive, and finally Hays' band drove them farther out west, and made them suffer so much after each of their raids that they talked of wanting peace, and thus it went on for several years.

On June 10, 1839, a party of Americans under Hays and a company of Mexicans under Captain Juan N. Seguin set off in pursuit of the Comanches, who just then were very bold, and were constantly killing and scalping and robbing in every direction. The Indians fled and were chased into the Canyon de Uvalde, where our men found and destroyed their villages, newly deserted. They saw numbers of Indians all the time in the distance, amongst rocks and hills, but scattered and hiding or fleeing from danger. They had been away from San Antonio ten days, when Captain Seguin returned reporting the woods full of Indians and predicting that our men would surely be killed. Mr. Maverick was with Hays, and after five more terribly anxious days, I was gladdened by his return. Our men had killed only a few savages and returned with some Indian ponies, dreadfully ragged, dirty and hungry.

At the close of the Fall Term of the Court in 1839 or 1840, a number of gentlemen who had attended from a distance, wished to ride out to the west of town and see the country before they returned home. A party was made up of ten Americans and about as many Mexicans. They were well mounted and armed and rode out about three o'clock in the afternoon. After sunset, Mr. Campbell, "Talking Campbell," one of the party, returned alone and reported the Indians had got between the party and town, cut off retreat, and killed all but himself, who rode a very fine horse and had fled at once; he advised the others, he said, to cut their way back because the Indians greatly outnumbered our party. Campbell was hotly pursued by the Indians, and he made a detour to the south, where his horse distanced the pursuers finally, and he came into town with the dreadful news. Next morning, early, a strong party left town with carts, and by noon returned with eighteen bodies. They were taken to the Court House and laid out. They had been found naked, hacked with tomahawks and partly eaten by wolves. The following day, the nine Americans were buried in one large grave west of the San Pedro, outside of the Catholic burying ground, and very near its S. W. corner. The nine Mexicans were buried inside the Catholic cemetery. It was believed some Indians had been killed too, but as they always carried off their dead, their loss was never ascertained.

In the spring of 1840, my brothers William and Andrew Adams leased land of J. A. de la Garza, at the mission of San Francisco de la Espada, and put in a crop. But the Indians were so bad, and corn so dear, selling then at two or three dollars per bushel, and their plow animals were so constantly stolen, that they broke up in the fall, and moved to San Marcos, and bought land of a Mr. Mathews, where they made fine crops for two years.

A DAY OF HORRORS.

On Tuesday, 19th of March, 1840, "dia de San Jose" sixty-five Comanches came into town to make a treaty of peace. They brought with them, and reluctantly gave up, Matilda Lockhart, whom they had captured with her younger sister in December 1838, after killing two other children of her family. The Indian chiefs and men met in council at the Court House, with our city and military authorities. The calaboose or jail then occupied the corner formed by the east line of Main Plaza and the north line of Calabosa (now Market) Street, and the Court House was north of and adjoining the jail. The Court House yard, back of the Court House, was what is now the city market on Market Street. The Court House and jail were of stone, one story, flat roofed, and floored with dirt. Captain Tom Howard's Company was at first in the Court House yard, where the Indian women and boys came and remained during the pow-wow. The young Indians amused themselves shooting arrows at pieces of money put up by some of the Americans; and Mrs. Higginbotham and myself amused ourselves looking through the picket fence at them.

This was the third time these Indians had come for a talk, pretending to seek peace, and trying to get ransom money for their American and Mexican captives. Their proposition now was that they should be paid a great price for Matilda Lockhart, and a Mexican they had just given up, and that traders be sent with paint, powder, flannel, blankets and such other articles as they should name, to ransom the other captives. This course had once before been asked and carried out, but the smallpox breaking out, the Indians killed the traders and kept the goods—believing the traders had made the smallpox to kill them. Now the Americans, mindful of the treachery of the Comanches, answered them as follows: "We will according to a former agreement,* keep four or five of your chiefs, whilst the others of your people go to your

---

*With Chief Muc Warrak.

nation and bring all the captives, and then we will pay all you ask for them. Meanwhile, these chiefs we hold we will treat as brothers and 'not one hair of their heads shall be injured.' This we have determined, and, if you try to fight, our soldiers will shoot you down."

This being interpreted, the Comanches instantly, with one accord raised a terrific war-whoop, drew their arrows, and commenced firing with deadly effect, at the same time making efforts to break out of the council hall. The order "fire" was given by Captain Howard, and the soldiers fired into the midst of the crowd, the first volley killing several Indians and two of our own people. All soon rushed out into the public square, the civilians to procure arms, the Indians to flee, and the soldiers in pursuit. The Indians generally made for the river—they ran up Soledad, east on Commerce Street and for the bend, now known as Bowen's, southeast, below the square. Citizens and soldiers pursued and overtook them at all points, shot some swimming in the river, had desperate fights in the streets—and hand to hand encounters after firearms had been exhausted. Some Indians took refuge in stone houses and fastened the doors. Not one of the sixty-five Indians escaped—thirty-three were killed and thirty-two were taken prisoners. Six Americans and one Mexican were killed and ten Americans wounded. Our killed were Julian Hood, the sheriff, Judge Thompson, advocate from South Carolina, G. W. Cayce from the Brazos, one officer and two soldiers whose names I did not learn, nor that of the Mexican. The wounded were Lieutenant Thompson, brother of the Judge, Captain Tom Howard, Captain Mat Caldwell, citizen volunteer from Gonzales, Judge Robinson, Mr. Morgan, deputy sheriff, Mr. Higginbotham and two soldiers. Others were slightly wounded.

When the deafening war-whoop sounded in the Court room, it was so loud, so shrill and so inexpressibly horrible and suddenly raised, that we women looking through the fence at the women's and boy's markmanship for a moment could not comprehend its purport. The Indians how-

ever knew the first note and instantly shot their arrows
into the bodies of Judge Thompson and the other gentleman near by, instantly killing Judge Thompson. We fled
into Mrs. Higginbotham's house and I, across the street
to my Commerce Street door. Two Indians ran past me on
the street and one reached my door as I got in. He turned
to raise his hand to push it just as I beat down the heavy
bar; then he ran on. I ran in the north room and saw my
husband and brother Andrew sitting calmly at a table in-
specting some plats of surveys—they had heard nothing.
I soon gave them the alarm, and hurried on to look for my
boys. Mr. Maverick and Andrew seized their arms, always ready—Mr. Maverick rushed into the street, and
Andrew into the back yard where I was shouting at the
top of my voice "Here are Indians!" "Here are Indians!"
Three Indians had gotten in through the gate on Soledad
street and were making direct for the river! One had
paused near Jinny Anderson, our cook, who stood bravely in front of the children, mine and hers, with a great
rock lifted in both hands above her head, and I heard
her cry out to the Indian "If you don't go 'way from
here I'll mash your head with this rock!" The Indian
seemed regretful that he hadn't time to dispatch Jinny
and her brood, but his time was short, and pausing
but a moment, he dashed down the bank into the river.
and struck out for the opposite shore.

As the Indian hurried down the bank and into the river
Andrew shot and killed him, and shot another as he gain-
ed and rose on the opposite bank,—then he ran off up
Soledad street looking for more Indians.

I housed my little ones, and then looked out of the Soledad Street door. Near by was stretched an Indian,
wounded and dying. A large man, journey-apprentice to
Mr. Higginbotham, came up just then and aimed a pistol
at the Indian's head. I called out: "Oh, don't, he is
dying," and the big American laughed and said: "To
please you, I won't, but it would put him out of his
misery." Then I saw two others lying dead near by.

Captain Lysander Wells, about this time, passed by riding north on Soledad Street. He was elegantly dressed and mounted on a gaily caparisoned Mexican horse with silver mounted saddle and bridle—which outfit he had secured to take back to his native state, on a visit to his mother. As he reached the Verimendi House, an Indian who had escaped detection, sprang up behind him, clasped Wells' arms in his and tried to catch hold of the bridle reins. Wells was fearless and active. They struggled for some time, bent back and forward, swayed from side to side, till at last Wells held the Indian's wrists with his left hand, drew his pistol from the holster, partly turned, and fired into the Indian's body—a moment more and the Indian rolled off and dropped dead to the ground. Wells then put spurs to his horse which had stood almost still during the struggle, dashed up the street and did good service in the pursuit. I had become so fascinated by this struggle that I had gone into the street almost breathless, and wholly unconscious of where I was, till recalled by the voice of Lieutenant Chavallier who said: "Are you crazy? Go in or you will be killed." I went in but without feeling any fear, though the street was almost deserted and my husband and brother both gone in the fight. I then looked out on Commerce street and saw four or five dead Indians. I was just twenty-two then, and was endowed with a fair share of curiosity.

Not till dark did all our men get back, and I was grateful to God, indeed, to see my husband and brother back alive and not wounded.

Captain Mat Caldwell, or "Old Paint," as he was familiarly called, our guest from Gonzales, was an old and famous Indian fighter. He had gone from our house to the Council Hall unarmed. But when the fight began, he wrenched a gun from an Indian and killed him with it, and beat another to death with the butt end of the gun. He was shot through the right leg, wounded as he thought by the first volley of the soldiers. After breaking the gun, he then fought with rocks, with his back to the Court House wall.

Young G. W. Cayce had called on us that morning,

'92. Sept. 1842 Lewis — typhoid fever was dangerously ill with fever then prevalent in the neighbourhood. Our slave Griffin had come back from S.A. & was greatly troubled about his master, to whom he was much attached, I called him to me, & talked with him about going out to Set. to pass himself for a run-away, follow to Mexico, & do anything he could to free, or even to aid S.A.M. & he should have his freedom. He answered that to do anything for his master would delight him, & he had been wanting to ask me to let him go — "as for my freedom he added I do not want any more than I have, master has always treated me more like a brother than a slave", & he choked up unable to say more. He took a gun, a good mule, some money, & made ready & started within a few hours — happy to think he might do something to help his master. 16th Juan Seguin killed Dr Smithers, McDonald, & McKhrea, at the Sulphur Springs on the Cibolo. 17th 163 men under Col Mat Caldwell are on the Cibolo going west.. 18th Caldwell moved with 225 men to the Salado, & on the morning of the 19th selecting a ravine for his force, he ordered Hays with 50 mounted men to draw

bringing an introductory letter from his father to Mr. Maverick, and placing some papers in his charge. He was a very pleasant and handsome young man and it was reported, came to marry Gertrudes Navarro, Mrs. Dr. Allsbury's sister. He left our house when I did, I going to Mrs. Higginbotham's and he to the Council Hall. He stood in the front door of the Court House, was shot and instantly killed at the beginning of the fight, and fell by the side of Captain Caldwell. The brother of this young man afterwards told me he had left home with premonition of his death being very near. Captain Caldwell was assisted back to our house and Dr. Weideman came and cut off his boot and found the bullet had gone entirely through the leg, and lodged in the boot, where it was discovered. The wound, though not dangerous, was very painful, but the doughty Captain recovered rapidly and in a few days walked about with the aid of a stick.

After the captain had been cared for, I ran across to Mrs. Higginbotham's. Mr. Higginbotham, who was as peaceful as a Quaker to all appearances, had been in the fight and had received a slight wound. They could not go into their back yard, because two Indians had taken refuge in their kitchen, and refused to come out or surrender as prisoners when the interpreter had summoned them.

A number of young men took counsel together that night, and agred upon a plan. Anton Lockmar and another got on the roof, and, about two hours after midnight dropped a candlewick ball soaked in turpentine, and blazing, through a hole in the roof upon one Indian's head and so hurt him and frightened them both that they opened the door and rushed out—to their death. An axe split open the head of one of the Indians before he was well out of the door, and the other was killed before he had gone many steps—thus the last of the sixty-five were taken. The Indian women dressed and fought like the men, and could not be told apart. As I have said thirty-three were killed and thirty-two taken prisoners. Many of them were repeatedly summoned to surrender, but numbers refused and were killed. All had a chance to surrender, and every one who offered or agreed to give up was taken prisoner and protected.

What a day of horrors! And the night was as bad which followed.

Lieutenant Thompson, who had been shot through the lungs, was taken to Madam Santita's house, on Soledad Street, just opposite us, and that night he vomited blood and cried and groaned all night—I shall never forget his gasping for breath and his agonizing cries. Dr. Weideman sat by and watched him, or only left to see the other sufferers, nearby; no one thought he would live till day, but he did, and got to be well and strong again, and in a few weeks walked out.

The captive Indians were all put in the calaboose for a few days and while they were there our forces entered into a twelve days truce with them—the captives acting for their Nation. And, in accordance with the stipulations of the treaty, one of the captives, an Indian woman, widow of a chief, was released on the 20th, the day after the fight. She was given a horse and provisions and sent to her Nation to tell her people of the fight and its result. She was charged to tell them, in accordance with the truce, to bring in all their captives, known to be fifteen Americans and several Mexicans, and exchange them for the thirty-two Indians held. She seemed eager to effect this, and promised to do her best. She said she would travel day and night, and could go and return within five days. The other prisoners thought she could in five days return with the captives from the tribe. The Americans said "very well we give twelve days truce and if you do not get back by Thursday night of the 28th, these prisoners shall be killed, for we will know you have killed our captive friends and relatives."

In April, as I shall mention again, we were informed by a boy, named B. L. Webster, that when the squaw reached her tribe and told of the disaster, all the Comanches howled, and cut themselves with knives, and killed horses, for several days. And they took all the American captives, thirteen in number, and roasted and butchered them to death with horrible cruelties; that he and a little girl named Putman, five years old, had been spared because they had previously been adopted into the tribe. Our people did not, however, retaliate upon the captives in our hands. The captive Indians were all put into the calaboose, corner Market Street and the public square and adjoining the courthouse, where all the people in San Antonio went to see them. The Indians expected to be killed, and they did not understand nor trust the kindness which was shown them and the great pity manifested toward them. They were first removed to San José Mission, where a company of soldiers was stationed, and afterwards taken to Camp "Cook," named after W. G. Cook, at the head of the river, and strictly guarded for a time. But afterwards the strictness was relaxed, and they gradually all, except a few, who were exchanged, escaped and returned to their tribe. They were kindly treated and two or three of them were taken into families as domestics, and were taught some little, but they too, at last, silently stole away to their ancient freedom.

Chapter VII.

DOCTOR WEIDEMAN.

LATE in the afternoon of the Indian fight, of the 19th, I visited Mrs. Higginbotham's, as I have before stated. While I was there, Dr. Weideman came up to her grated front window, and placed a severed Indian head upon the sill. The good doctor bowed courteously and saying, "With your permission, Madam," disappeared. Soon after he returned with another bloody head, when he explained to us that he had viewed all the dead Indians, and selected these two heads, male and female, for the skulls, and also had selected two entire bodies, male and female, to preserve as specimen skeletons. He said: "I have been long exceedingly anxious to secure such specimens—and now, ladies, I must hurry and get a cart to take them to my house," and off he hurried all begimed with dirt and blood, (having been with his good horse one of the foremost in pursuit.) Now he was exulting for the cause of science in his "magnificent specimens" and before it was quite dark, he came with his cart and its frightful load, took his two heads and disappeared. His house was the old Chaves place, on the side of Acequia Street, (now Main Avenue,) north of Main Plaza. Dr. Weideman, a Russian, was a very learned man of perhaps thirty-five years of age, was a surgeon and M. D., spoke many living tongues and had travelled very extensively. In former years, he had buried a lovely young wife and son, and becoming resless, had sought and secured employment under the Russian Government. In fact the Emperor of Russia had sent him to Texas to find and report anything and everything, vegetable and animal grown in Texas—and he had selected a

worthy man, for Dr. Weideman was a devotee to science.
He grew enthusiastic over our Western Texas and her climate and constantly accompanied the "Minute Men" on
their expeditions and numerous surveying parties.

Dr. Weideman took the Indian heads and bodies to his
home as I have mentioned, and put them into a large
soap boiler on the bank of the "esequia," or ditch, which
ran in front of his premises. During the night of the 20th
he emptied the boiler, containing water and flesh from
the bones, into the ditch. Now this ditch furnished the
drinking water generally for the town. The river and the
San Pedro Creek, it was understood, were for bathing
and washing purposes, but a city ordinance prohibited,
with heavy fines, the throwing of any dirt or filth into
the ditch—for it was highly necessary and proper to keep
the drinking water pure.

On the 21st, it dawned upon the dwellers upon the
banks of the ditch that the doctor had defiled their drinking water. "There arose a great hue and cry and
all the people crowded to the mayor's office—the men
talked in loud and excited tones, the women shrieked
and cried—they rolled up their eyes in horror, they vomited, and many thought they were poisoned and must die.
Dr. Weideman was arrested and brought to trial, he was
overwhelmed with abuse, he was called "diabolo," "de-
monio." "sin verguenza," etc., etc. He took it quite
calmly, told the poor creatures they would not be hurt—
that the Indian poison had all run off with the water long
before day—paid his fine and went off laughing.

The doctor had a Mexican servant who had been pretty
good, and lived with him two years—but Jose would
steal—and one day he stole the doctor's watch, a valuable gold timepiece. Dr. Weideman after inquiring and
waiting several weeks in vain, determined to have his
watch, if he had to use magic to get it. He had several
Mexican men servants, for he kept horses, wild animals,
snakes and birds and also cultivated a fine garden—with
wild flowers, etc., he satisfied himself that Jose was

the thief. He invited several gentlemen to come to his house a certain evening about full of the moon, and he told his servants that he would summon the spirits to point out the thief· When the appointed time came, he caused a fire to be built on the flat dirt roof of his house, over which he placed a pot filled with liquids. Hither he brought his company and the servants. He was dressed in a curious robe or gown covered with weird figures, and a tall wonderful cap rested on his head. In his hand he held a twisted stick· with which he stirred the liquid in the pot uttering the while words in an unknown tongue. He was very solemn and occasionally he would turn around slowly and gaze upward into space. Finally he told all present that he would put out the fire, and cool the liquid, and then each person in turn should dip his hand in, and the thief's hand would turn black. Each one advanced in due order and submitted his hand to the test, and after each experiment the doctor would stir and mutter and turn around again. Jose waited until the very last, he came up quite unwillingly, and when he withdrew his hand from the pot it was black. Jose was terribly frightened, he fell upon his knees and acknowledged the theft then and there and begged for mercy. The Doctor got his watch back and did not discharge Jose, who never after stole again.

The Mexicans when they saw the doctor on the streets would cross themselves, and avoid him—they said he was leagued with the devil; he claimed that the spirits of the Indians, whose bodies he had dissected, were under his enchantment and that he could make them tell him anything. He set his skeleton Indians up in his garden, in his summer house, and dared anybody to steal on his premises. It is needless to say, everything he had was sacred from theft.

Dr. Weideman was very good to the sick and wounded. He would not take pay for his services, and saved many lives by his skill and attention. He was universally respected and liked by the Americans. In 1843 or '44 he was drowned in attempting to cross Peach Creek, near

Gonzales when the water was very high—his horse and himself and one other man were carried down by the rapid current and drowned, whilst the others of the party barely escaped.

During the summer of this year, 1840, Colonel Henry Karnes* upon returning from Houston when yellow fever was prevailing there, was taken down with yellow fever. The Colonel and Dr. Weideman were great friends, and the Doctor hardly left his room till he was out of danger. Karnes thought though his business required him in Houston, and contrary to the doctor's advice, he started back before he was strong enough. He travelled stretched out in a light wagon—took a relapse after the first day and came back to his friends. But his case was now hopeless, and he died from his great imprudence, and the good doctor put on the deepest mourning for his friend. Colonel Karnes was a short, thick-set man with bright red hair. While he was uneducated, he was modest, generous and devoted to his friends. He was brave and untiring and a terror to the Indians. They called him "Capitan Colorado" (Red Captain) and spoke of him as "Muy Wapo" (very brave.) Four or five years before he died, he was taken prisoner by the Comanches, and the squaws so greatly admired his hair of "fire" that they felt it and washed it to see if it would fade; and, when they found the color held fast, they would not be satisfied until each had a lock.

---

*Karnes came from Tennessee and joined the Texas forces at Conception '35, while very young. Yoakum refers to an amusing incident of this same battle. "One who was often with him, (Karnes), and by his side at Conception, says he never knew him to swear before or since that day. But when he came into the lines, after being shot at so often, and began to load his rifle, he exclaimed with some wrath, 'The d——d rascals have shot out the bottom of my powder horn.' Karnes was quite sober and temperate . . . he had remarkable gentleness and delicacy of feeling."

Chapter VIII.
COMANCHES AND A DUEL.

ISIMANICA. Several incidents occurred soon after the fight of the 19th, which, together with other incidents much later, I will narrate.

On March 28th between two hundred and fifty and three hundred Comanches under a dashing young chief, Isimanica, came close to the edge of the town where the main body halted and chief Isimanica with another warrior rode daringly into the public square, and circled around it, then rode some distance down Commerce Street and back, shouting all the while, offering fight and heaping abuse and insults upon the Americans. Isimanica was in full war paint, and almost naked. He stopped longest at Black's saloon, at the north east corner of the square; he shouted defiance, he rose in his stirrups, shook his clenched fist, raved, and foamed at the mouth. The citizens, through an interpreter, told him the soldiers were all down the river at Mission San Jose and if he went there Colonel Fisher would give him fight enough.

Isimanica took his braves to San Jose,* and with fearless daring bantered the soldiers for a fight. Colonel Fisher was lying on a sick bed and Captain Redd, the next in rank, was in command. He said to the chief: "We have made a twelve day truce with your people in order to exchange prisoners. My country's honor is pledged, as well as my own, to keep the truce, and I will not break it.

---

*Mission San José, (St. Joseph), or Second Mission, named also for the Governor of the province of Texas at the time, "de Aguayo," was founded in 1720— and completed about 1730 the same year Mission Conception was begun.

San José is said by many to be the most beautiful of all the Missions in this country—though it has been badly neglected, and the wonderful carvings broken and defaced by relic hunters.

The South window of the Baptistry is considered by good judges the finest gem of architectural ornamentation existing in America today." Wm. Corner S. A. de Bexar. (See cover sketch.)

LEWIS ANTONIO MAVERICK

Remain here three days or return in three days and the truce will be over. We burn to fight you." Isimanica called him liar, coward and other opprobrious names, and hung around for some time, but at last the Indians left and did not return. Captain Redd remained calm and unmoved, but his men could with the greatest difficulty be restrained, and in fact some of them were ordered into the Mission church and the door guarded.

When Captain Lysander Wells, a non-commissioned officer, who was in town, heard of it, he wrote Captain Redd an insulting letter in which he called him a "dastardly coward," and alluded to a certain "petticoat goverment" under which he intimated the Captain was restrained. This allusion had reference to a young woman who, dressed in boy's apparel, had followed Redd from Georgia and was now living with him. This letter of Wells' was signed, much to their shame, by several others in San Antonio. About this time Colonel Fisher removed his entire force of three companies to the Alamo in San Antonio; Redd challenged Wells to mortal combat, and one morning at six o'clock they met where the Ursuline Convent now stands. Redd said: "I aim for your heart," and Wells answered: "And I for your brains." They fired. Redd sprang high into the air and fell dead with a bullet in his brain. Wells was shot near the heart, but lived two weeks, in great torture, begging every one near him to dispatch him, or furnish him a pistol that he might kill himself and end his agony; Dr. Weideman nursed him tenderly. In Captain Redd's pocket was found a marriage license and certificate showing that he was wedded to the girl (before mentioned)—also letters to members of his own and her families, speaking of her in the tenderest manner, and asking them to protect and provide for her. She was heartbroken and went to his funeral in black . . and soon returned to her family.

These men were both brave and tried soldiers! What a sad ending to their young and promising lives, and that too, when cruel and relentless savages daily committed atrocities about us.

Captives.   Matilda Lockhart, who came in as I have mentioned, on March 19th, had been about two years in captivity.   When she was captured, two of her family were slain, and she and her little sister were taken prisoners.   At that time she was thirteen and her sister not three years of age.   They were taken off to the tribe. Just before her release, she came along with the Indian party, as a herder, driving a herd of extra ponies for the Indians.   The Indians thus could exchange their horses from time to time for fresher ones.

She was in a frightful condition, poor girl, when at last she returned to civilization. Her head, arms and face were full of bruises, and sores, and her nose actually burnt off to the bone—all the fleshy end gone, and a great scab formed on the end of the bone.   Both nostrils were wide open and denuded of flesh.   She told a piteous tale of how dreadfully the Indians had beaten her, and how they would wake her from sleep by sticking a chunk of fire to her flesh, especially to her nose, and how they would shout and laugh like fiends when she cried.   Her body had many scars from fire, many of which she showed us. Ah, it was sickening to behold, and made one's blood boil for vengeance.

Matilda was now fifteen years old, and, though glad to be free from her detested tyrants, she was very sad and broken hearted.   She said she felt utterly degraded, and could never hold her head up again—that she would be glad to get back home again, where she would hide away and never permit herself to be seen.   How terrible to comtemplate! Yet her case was by no means solitary. She told of fifteen other American captives, all children, then in the Nation, and two adopted captives, her little sister and Booker Webster.   After a few days, Matilda's brother came and took her home.

On March 26th, Mrs. Webster came in with her three year old child on her back.   This poor miserable being was hailed by the excited Mexicans as "India," "India," as she trudged along to the center of the town.   She came into the Public Square from the west, and was dressed as an Indian in buckskin. Like the Indians, her hair was cut short and square upon her forehead, and she was sunburned and as dark as a Comanche.

She called out in good English, however, and said she had escaped from Indian captivity. She was taken into John W. Smith's house, and we American ladies soon gathered there to see her and attend her wants. She said she was very tired and hungry and appeared much exhausted. After listening to a part of her story, Mrs. Smith gave her some food, which she and her little one ate in a famished manner. Five of us ladies, Mrs. Jacques, Mrs. Elliott, Mrs. Smith, Mrs. Higginbotham and myself, agreed to unite in caring for the unhappy fugitives. We got her some clothing, and, having prepared a bath, we helped her to undress and found her skin yet fair and white beneath the buckskin. We bathed and clothed her and left her to sleep and rest.

The stench of the poor woman's clothes was so dreadful, while we were undressing her, that Mrs. Jacques fainted away, and Mrs. Smith told me to get a bottle of cologne on her mantel in the adjoining room. I picked up the only bottle there, and hastily sprinkled the contents on Mrs. Jacques's face, which caused her to revive instantly, and she screamed: "Stop, stop, that is pepper vinegar!," And so it was indeed, and had gotten into one of her eyes, whereupon Mrs. Jacques was accused of "playing 'possum," and we had a great laugh. Mrs. Webster remained a week with Mrs. Smith, a week with Mrs. Jacques and two weeks with us. She was treated with great kindness by every one, and money and clothes given her. Her story was as follows:—

She came from Virginia to Texas early in 1838 with her husband, who she claimed, was a relative of Daniel Webster. They built a house northwest of Austin, and in August of that year her husband was removing her and her four children to this wild home—they had also in the party two negroes and one white man. One evening they camped on Brushy Creek, not far north of Austin, when a large party of Comanches suddenly attacked

them. Their three men fought bravely, but were over-
powered and killed. Mrs. Webster's infant was taken
from her arms, and its brains dashed out on a tree and her
second child was killed. She and her eldest boy of ten
years, Brooker Webster, were tied upon horses, and she
held her child of two years so tightly and plead for it so
piteously, that the Indians left it with her. They were
taken by rapid marches to the mountains, where they
stripped Booker and shaved his head. He was attacked
with brain fever, and an old squaw, who had just lost a
son of his age, adopted him and nursed him very tenderly.
The Indians allowed Mrs. Webster to keep her little girl,
but prohibited her from talking with her son. They made
her cook, and stake out ponies, and they beat her very
badly. She had been nineteen months in captivity when
she seized a favorable opportunity to escape. It was one
night after a long day's march when, having learned the
general direction of San Antonio, she quietly and noise-
lessly slipped out of camp with her child in her arms,
and bent her steps toward Bexar. She spent twelve terrible days on the road without meeting a human being—
sustaining herself all this while on berries, small fish
which she caught in the streams, and bones left at Indian
camps, which she followed, hiding and sleeping in the
day, and travelling at night by moon and starlight. She
several times gave up to die, but gathering courage and
determination, she would trudge on. The early morning of
the 26th she lay down despairing on a hillside in a fog,
not able to drag one foot after the other. When the sun
shone out, looking to the east she saw a "golden cross
shining in the sky!" Then she knew her prayers had been
answered and that cross surmounted the Cathedral of San
Fernando in San Antonio. She said she felt her weariness
melt away and she grew strong and hopeful and again
took up the march with a thankful heart. She was about
thirty-two years old.

April 3rd. Two Indians, a chief and a squaw, the man
with his bow strung and arrows in his hand, came into
the public square and, remaining mounted, called out to

the Americans that about twenty warriors were holding all the American and Mexican captives three miles from town, and that they were prepared to make the exchange proposed or agreed upon in the twelve days' truce. The Amerirans sent scouts, who reported the Indians to be numerous and the captives few. Two companies of soldiers and nine captive Indians were ordered up from San Jose. The Americans declined to go with the chief to the Indian camp, but they gave him bread, peloncillos and a beef and agreed to talk "manana," (tomorrow.)

On the 4th, the chief returned and asked the Americans to take out two captives and exchange for two, and the answer was: "Bring two captives to the edge of town and we will meet you." They came with a little American girl, Putman's child, and a Mexican boy, and received two Indians. The Americans being desirous of securing all the captives, not knowing they were murdered, asked why they did not bring American captives, and the Indians answered they had only one more with them, and if they gave him up they wished to choose an Indian in exchange. The boy proved to be B. L. Webster, "Booker," the son of Mrs. Webster mentioned above, and they brought a Mexican boy with him and said these were all they had with them. The chief selected in exchange for Webster a squaw whose arm had been broken in the fight of the 19th. When asked why he chose her, he answered she was the widow of a great chief who had been killed in the fight, and he wanted her for his squaw, because she owned "muchas mules," "muchas mules." The squaw did not seem to relish this and so the Americans would not let him take her, but selected another woman, and a child, and threw in a blind Indian. The chief was not pleased, but departed with what he could get.

Thus we got back two American and five Mexican captives. Booker Webster's head was shaved and he was painted in Indian style. One of the Mexicans ran away some time afterwards and returned to the Indians. The girl, Putman, was five years old, and cried to go back to the Comanche mother who had adopted her, probably in her second year. She could not speak or understand English, and had many bruises and her nose was burnt partly off. The boy, Booker, then told us, and we learnt for the first time, how the Comanches had murdered the captives in their hands when they received the message borne to them by the squaw.

The Indians used the Spanish language a great deal, but they never tried to acquire any knowledge of the English tongue. This summer, 1840, the Indians were constantly stealing and murdering. Travel was especially unsafe, except when the company was large, and even then it was advisable to travel by night and camp by day, always keeping a sharp lookout.

Indian Raid to Lavaca Bay.   Early in August, a band of about three hundred warriors suddenly appeared in the neighborhood of Victoria, having escaped detection on their route down the country. On the 6th, they appeared there in force.   Circling around Victoria, they passed on to Linnville, a small town on Lavaca Bay, one and a quarter miles below the present site of Lavaca. Linnville was a very small town in which was located a Custom House and a few stores. When the Indians charged into the town, most of the citizens took refuge on the boats anchored near, and thus escaped. Some were not quick enough, and were cut off and killed, and two ladies and a boy were taken prisoners. The Indians found large quantities of goods stored at Linnville which they loaded upon pack animals, and even upon their riding horses. They spent the whole day there, and burnt all the houses and everything they could not carry off.   Meanwhile, runners had been sent out of Victoria to warn the settlers, and for the purpose of summoning volunteers to intercept the Indians' return to the mountains. The call was responded to from every valley and settlement. From the Colorado to the Guadalupe and beyond, volunteers gathered, under McColloch, Lynn, Caldwell, Ed Burleson, Moore and others. Scouts who followed close upon their trail told of whole bolts of ribbon, muslin and calico streaming to the air from the saddles of the savages.   On

Plum Creek, a branch of the San Marcos, August 18th, they were at last surrounded, retreat cut off and they forced to fight. The Texas forces, under general Felix Houston, had been gathering for one grand blow. The combat was remarkable for the terrible slaughter of the Indians. The battle ground extended over a distance of fifteen miles, for it was a running fight. None of the Texans were killed, and the Indians were so completely crushed by this defeat that they never dared to raid into that section again.

When they found they would lose the fight, the Indians lanced and shot arrows into their captives, who were tied to trees, and left them for dead, but Mrs. Watts recovered and returned to her friends. The capture of Mrs. Watts illustrates how vitally important a few moments of time may become. Mr. Watts had married this lady only a few weeks before the Comanches burned Linnville, and had presented her with an elegant gold watch and chain. After starting to run for the boats, Mrs. Watts thought she would secure her watch first, ran back into the house, and got it, accompanied by her husband. Having secured the trinket, they attempted to reach the boats, but some mounted Indians had cut them off. Watts was tomahawed, and his wife taken captive. She afterwards married again to a Mr. Staunton, I am told, and died at Lavaca in 1878.

Now, why have I mentioned this raid? Well you shall hear. On April 21st, Mr. Maverick had left for New Orleans and returned in June by the way of Houston. He had only got home a week before this, and had intended to come by Lavaca, but was detained. He however, shipped by way of Linnville, goods, stores and a supply of clothing material for two years ahead, and unfortunately for us the goods were stored in Linnville when the Indians sacked the place. Mr. Maverick had purchased a supply of whiskey and brandy to be used on surveying expeditions —it being the custom for those having surveying done to furnish the liquor. He had purchased for me a silver soup ladle, twelve table and twelve tea spoons; the spoons we had travelled out with were only plated ware. He had also a number of law books with the other things. These law books were the only things we ever heard from, and what he heard was this: they were strung to the Indians' saddles by strings run through the volumes, and used for making cigarettes.*

I shall not mention the thousand and one incidents which happened in connection with the Comanches in and about San Antonio from 1838 until 1842, when we became refugees. They made life very unsafe on the frontier and during the period mentioned they were always within dangerous proximity to us and always doing some of their devilment.

However I will mention one or two more incidents before I bid them adieu. On May 27th, thirty or forty Comanches came close to town, and being early discovered, they were hotly pursued by the "Minute Men." They fled to the nearest timber on the Medina, where, darkness overtaking them, they speared all their horses and took to the bottom on foot. In the morning, the dead horses were found but the Indians had escaped·

The Indians were always lurking around in small bodies hiding close to town, waiting for an opportunity to strike without danger to themselves. We were compelled to learn this through many murders and robberies. They would suddenly appear from the river bottom, from behind a clump of trees, from a gully, and sometimes from the tall grass. It seemed they were always on the watch everywhere, but only acted at the most favorable moments.

In the spring of 1841, Mrs. Elliott and I set out up the river to gather dewberries. They grew in great abundance where the Ursuline Convent now stands.* Mr. Elliott sent his two clerks, Peter·Gallagher and John Conran, Mrs. Elliott's brother, along, they being well armed. We with my son Sam and Billy Elliott and the two nurses Rachael and Julia, took our buckets and started up directly after

---

*Which shows what respect the Indians had for Blackstone and the law. G. M. M.

*Then a wild-wood. Mary A. Maverick.

dinner. We found a great abundance of ripe luscious berries, ate all we wanted, filled our buckets, had a first-rate time and started home alright. We met just after we left the bend of the river a Mexican cartman going out to hopple his oxen on the fine grass we had just passed over. We had gone only a few hundred feet further, after passing the Mexican, when we heard all around us the sudden cry of "Indios," "Indios." Soon the alarm bell called to arms and we ran quickly home. The cartman we passed proved to be the victim—he was killed and scalped by the Comanches, who had been hiding close to us in the river timber when we were gathering the berries and having our good time just before. Our two armed guards on the watch had saved our lives. The Indians both escaped in the dark and we were grateful for the foresight of Mr. Elliott, and we learned a lesson never forgotten, for our foolhardy venturing.

Chapter IX.
FAMILY HISTORY RESUMED.

MR. Maverick was a most earnest and enthusiastic admirer of Western Texas, and firm believer in her future. He was constantly in ecstasies over the beautiful valleys, the rich soil, the charming climate. Often he would speak in glowing terms of the magnificent expanses of fertile hill and dale. What a grand home for the toilers of Europe, he would say. Along with his admiration, came the spirit of speculation in land—all men of strong imagination speculated deeply in land in those days. So brilliant and so realistic were his visions of the future, that in his mind's eye the future, ah, the far distant future, became the tomorrow of the dreamer. Tomorrow they will come—tomorrow the overcrowded of the cities, the wearied sons of toil will come, and will build up this magnificient country into a grand empire. But the future came not to him—in his lifetime he saw the toilers come across the sea, but they came not to Texas; they settled in the great North West, and there they built up the empires of which he had prophesied.

Mr. Maverick took the greatest delight in the surveying camp. He purchased many thousands of acres of land certificates, and he was out much of the time locating and surveying lands for himself and for friends, or at least planning expeditions. I will tell of a trip he made in the fall of 1839. He fitted out the party and went, according to my best recollection, to the Medina and San Geronimo. Before they started, Mexicans killed and jerked beef* at our place, and they had a busy time packing the

---

*Jerked beef: many an old timer declares to this day that the flavor of beef cut in thin strips and sun dried, can not be equalled. Not only was meat "jerked" to prepare it for long marches, but kitchen doors of the early days were sometimes supplied with iron hooks upon which newly purchased steaks were hung and cooked in the hot sun. School girls and boys of the 60's relished "jerked" beef in their lunch boxes.

animals the day they started. Mr. Lapham, the deputy
surveyor, a nice gentleman from Vermont, spent a week at
our house, waiting for the preparations to be completed.
When they departed, I exacted from my husband the
promise that he would return on a certain day. He kept
his word, although the work was not completed—he
came in accordance with his promise, and brought with
him one or two of the party. The very night after he left
the camp, the Indians surprised the camp and killed every
one, save one chain bearer, who escaped on a fine horse. A
party went out to bury the dead and found the compass
and papers and some other articles.

1840.

Mr. Maverick, as I have mentioned, left us for the
"States" April, 1840, and returned the latter part of June.
He went to Pendleton, South Carolina, when he was
away, but he told me, "I had not the face to go to Mother's without you and the boys—she would take it so to
heart."

Sept. 16th, The Mexicans celebrated Dia de Inde-
pendencia." On December 12th, the Mexicans celebrated
in grand procession "Dia de Nuestra Senora de Guadalupe," the patroness saint of Mexico , and whom the
priests had identified with the Virgin Mary. Twelve
young girls dressed in spotless white, bore a platform on
which stood a figure representing the saint very richly
and gorgeously dressed. First came the priests in procession, then the twelve girls bearing the platform, and carrying each in her free hand a lighted wax' candle, then
came fiddlers behind them playing on their violins, and
following the fiddlers the devout population, generally,
firing off guns and pistols and showing their devotion in
various ways. They proceeded through the squares and
some of the principal streets, and every now and then they
all knelt and repeated a short prayer—an "Ave Marie" or
"Pater Noster." Finally the procession stopped at the
Cathedral of San Fernando on the Main Plaza, where a
long ceremony was had. Afterwards the more prominent
families taking the Patroness along with them, adjourn-

ed to Mr. Jose Flores' house on west side of Military Plaza, where they danced most of the night. We were invited and went, taking with us little Sammy with his jolly golden curls and a new suit of pea green. It was all quite a novel and interesting scene to me.

The principal citizens lived in the plazas or within two blocks of them on Flores, Acequia, Soledad, Commerce and Market streets. Very few of the Mexican ladies could write but they dressed nicely and were graceful and gracious of manner. We exchanged calls with the Navarros, Sotos, Garzas, Garcias, Zambranos, Seguins, Veramendis and Yturris.

December 1840, Uncle John Bradley brought his family to San Antonio. They spent two or three weeks with us and then moved into the house formerly occupied by the Higginbothams, who had removed to the country. Annie Bradley was a lovely girl, very womanly and sweet tempered. About Christmas we attended a ball given at Chauncy Johnston's, who had brought out his family some two months before, and resided in the Casiano house. Annie received great attention and had a throng of admirers.

About this time Mr. Gautier, a French merchant, came to town with his wife and child.

1841.

We now began to have a society and great sociability amongst ourselves, the Americans. During the summer 1841, Mr. Wilson Riddle brought out his bride, and Mr. Moore his family. These gentlemen were both merchants on Commerce Street. Mr. Campbell married a second wife with whom and her sister, Miss O'Neill, he returned to San Antonio. Mr. Davis opened a store on Commerce Street. Mr. John Twohig started a small grocery store on corner of Commerce Street and Plaza Mayor.*

Mrs. Jacques had a boarding house at southwest

*Diaries were of real use on the frontier as records of events, for the daily paper did not exist, also as the mail or post was sent back to the States only once a month diaries were useful as reminders of interesting happenings to be chronicled in home letters.

corner of Commerce and Yturri—she had a whole block rented from Yturri and boarded all the nice young Americans, and was very hospitable and pleasant. She was a good nurse and extremely kind to any sick or wounded, and consequently a great favorite with the gentlemen. On Easter Sunday of this year, she invited all the American families, and many young gentlemen to dine with her. She served her dinner at the long room, (sagnan). She dinner was simply elegant, the company large and lively and we all enjoyed the day very much. In the afternoon we promenaded up Soledad Street in a gay and happy throng.

Easter Monday, April 12th, 1841, Agatha, our first daughter was born and named for my mother. She was a very beautiful and good baby.

My mother talked of coming out to visit us. Her idea was that she would come to some port on the coast, and we would go down at the appointed time and meet her there. But I had too many babies to make such a journey, and the risk from Indians was too great, and we did not encourage the plan. Her letters were one month to six weeks old when we received them.

President Lamar with a very considerable suite visited San Antonio in June. A grand ball was given him in Mrs. Yturri's long room—(all considerable houses had a long room for receptions). The room was decorated with flags and evergreens; flowers were not much cultivated then. At the ball, General Lamar wore very wide white pants which at the same time were short enough to show the tops of his shoes. General Lamar and Mrs. Juan N. Seguin, wife of the Mayor, opened the ball with a waltz. Mrs. Seguin was so fat that the General had great difficulty in getting a firm hold on her waist, and they cut such a figure that we were forced to smile. The General was a poet, a polite and brave gentleman and first rate conversationalist—but he did not dance well.

At the ball, Hays, Chevalier, and John Howard had but one dress coat between them, and they agreed to use the coat and dance in turn. The two not dancing would stand at the hall door watching the happy one who was enjoying his turn—and they reminded him when it was time for him to step out of that coat. Great fun was it watching them and listening to their wit and mischief as they made faces and shook their fists at the dancing one.

John D. Morris, the Adonis of the company, escorted Miss Arceneiga who on that warm evening wore a maroon cashmere with black plumes in her hair, and her haughty airs did not gain her any friends. Mrs. Yturri had a new silk, fitting her so tightly that she had to wear corsets for the first time in her life. She was very pretty, waltzed beautifully and was much sought as a partner. She was several times compelled to escape to her bedroom to take off the corset and "catch her breath", as she said to me who happened to be there with my baby.

By the way, speaking of Mrs. Yturri, I am reminded of a party I gave several months before this. It blew a freezing norther that day and we had the excellent good luck of making some ice cream, which was a grateful surprise to our guests. In fact those of the Mexicans present, who had never travelled, tasted ice cream that evening for the first time in their lives, and they all admired and liked it. But Mrs. Yturri ate so much of it, tho' advised not to, that she was taken with cramps. Mrs. Jacques and I took her to my room and gave her brandy, but in vain, and she had to be carried home. At that party some natives remained so late in the morning that we had to ask them to go. One man of reputable standing carried off a roast chicken in his pocket, another a carving knife, and several others took off all the cake they could well conceal, which greatly disgusted Jinny Anderson, the cook. Griffin followed the man with the carving knife and took it away from him.

During this summer, the American ladies led a lazy life of ease. We had plenty of books, including novels, we were all young, healthy and happy and were content with each others' society. We fell into the fashion of the climate, dined at twelve, then followed a siesta, (nap) until three, when we took a cup of coffee and a bath.

Bathing in the river at our place had become rather public, now that merchants were establishing themselves on Commerce Street, so we ladies got permission of old Madame Tevino, mother of Mrs. Lockmar, to put up a bath house on her premises, some distance up the river on Soledad Street, afterwards the property and homestead of the Jacques family. Here between two trees in a beautiful shade, we went in a crowd each afternoon at about four o'clock and took the children and nurses and a nice lunch which we enjoyed after the bath. There we had a grand good time, swimming and laughing, and making all the noise we pleased. The children were bathed and after all were dressed, we spread our lunch and enjoyed it immensely. The ladies took turns in preparing the lunch and my aunt Mrs. Bradley took the lead in nice things. Then we had a grand and glorious gossip, for we were all dear friends and each one told the news from our far away homes in the "States," nor did we omit to review the happenings in San Antonio. We joked and laughed away the time, for we were free from care and happy. In those days there were no envyings, no backbiting.

In September mother wrote she had determined to visit us, that she would leave Robert and Lizzie at school and that George would accompany her. William and Andrew were then on the San Marcos. She wrote she would set out about October first, and should she like our town she would sell out in Tuskaloosa and move to San Antonio. That letter arrived late in October, and soon after it came a letter from Professor Wilson to Mr. Maverick, and a letter from Mrs. Snow to me telling us that my dear mother was no more. She was taken with congestive chills—the first had been severe, but the second was light, and two weeks having elapsed after the second chill, Dr. Weir, her physician, considered her out of danger from a third. Lizzie had come home from school, and slept in the adjoining room, and a servant girl much attached to my mother slept on a pallet before mother's door. Mother would not allow any one to sit up with her now, and her tonic, lamp and watch were placed on a table near her. A third chill must have come on during the night, for by the early morning light, on October 2nd, they found that my dear mother was cold and dead. Oh, what a grief to me was this first great loss of my life. Her heart had been so set upon seeing me that I now blamed myself for not going to meet her at the coast when she had proposed it.

My mother had a sorrowful widowed life, for she was not always successful in managing business or in governing her boys. She blamed herself for her want of success as she called it, and she seldom smiled and never appeared to enjoy life. She was a devoted mother, but probably too strict with her children, and she was an humble,faithful Christian. Her death was to me a sudden awakening from a fancied security against all possible evil. Slowly and sadly I came to realize that my dear mother had left this world forever, and we should not meet again on earth.

President Lamar's visit to San Antonio in June was to sanction and encourage an expedition to Santa Fe, New Mexico. The object of this expedition was to open a line for commerce between the two sections, and get a share of the lucrative trade between Santa Fe and Lexington, Mo. Lamar gave the project his sanction and encouragement, furnished governmental supplies and sought the endorsement of Congress. He appointed William G. Cook, Don J. A. Navarro and R. F. Brenham commissioners to go with the expedition. The expedition, after much delay, set out from Brushy, near Georgetown, on the 20th of June, 1841. The party consisted of two hundred and seventy armed men under General Hugh McLeod, and fifty traders with wares and pack mules. There were also servants and some supernumeraries. Some of our brave young men of San Antonio were of the party. The unfortunate expedition, its total failure and the unhappy causes and consequences of the final disaster, are told with great vigor and fidelity by George W. Kendall who

MAVERICK HOMESTEAD, ALAMO PLAZA

MEXICAN HACAL WITH STRINGS OF BEEF DRYING
IN THE SUN

was of the party and wrote a thrilling history or narrative of the expedition.

It was strongly believed by many that Juan Nepomicino Seguin, who had held the honorable position of Mayor of San Antonio, and Representative to Congress, from Bexar, and being a man of great pride and ambition, had found himself surpassed by Americans, and somewhat overlooked in official places, had become dissatisfied with the Americans, and had opened communications with the officials of Mexico, exposing the entire plan from its inception as "invading Mexican soil." Certain it is that Governor Armijo of New Mexico was early advised of the expedition, and ordered to capture and put to death the whole party. From this time Seguin was suspected and Padre Garza, a rich and influential priest, was known to carry on traitorous correspondence with the Mexican authorities. Positive proof, however, was not obtained until Padre Garza escaped. Seguin indignantly denied the charge and many suspended judgement. His father, Don Erasmo Seguin, was a cultivated and enlightened man, who had befriended Stephen F. Austin in a Mexican dungeon, had been friendly to the Americans, and was much esteemed by all.

Chapter X.

FLIGHT.

DURING the fall of 1841 and the following winter, many rumors came to the effect that the Mexicans were about to invade Texas in force. Sometimes friendly-minded Mexicans dropped in to warn us and even to entreat us not to remain and be butchered, for they felt sure the invading army would be vindictive and cruel.

1842.

In February 1842, the scouts advised Captain Hays that a force had gathered on the right bank of the Rio Grande, had crossed to this side and was moving on toward San Antonio. We thought it must be a foraging party which would not venture into San Antonio, but our soldier friends insisted that the ladies and children should not remain any longer. The ladies finally agreed to move temporarily from San Antonio. Hasty preparations were made, and on March 1st, 1842, our little band started on the trip which we have always spoken of since as the "Runaway of '42."

Mrs. Campbell and Mrs. Moore waited a few days and did not afterwards overtake us. Mrs. Riddle had a two weeks old baby, (now Mrs. Eager), and could not move.

Our party consisted of Mrs. Elliott, three children and two servants; Mrs. Jacques, two children and one servant, also having Mr. Douglas, an invalid gentleman, in charge; Mrs. Bradley, six children and seven or eight servants; Messrs. Bradley, Jacques and Elliott having remained behind to pack up and urge forward such of their goods as were most valuable. In the party was also Mr. Gautier, wife and child, Judge Hutchinson and wife in their car-

riage with driver, the only fine carriage in the caravan—
and last but not least the tribe of Maverick. Mr. Maverick
and I were mounted, as also our two servants Griffin and
Wiley. Granville drove the wood cart drawn by two
horses, which carried Jinny, Rachael and quite a number
of children white and black. In the cart we had also the
necessary clothing, bedding and provisions. Our carriage
got out of repair soon after we settled in San Antonio, and
the wheel of our big Kentucky wagon was broken and we
found no blacksmith in the place able to mend or repair
either, so it will appear we were just a lttle crowded.
Mr. Maverick thought we would go back very soon, and
we left the house as it was with some gentlemen who
would live there and care for it. We buried some articles
under the storeroom floor and I left a bureau of drawers
in the care of Mrs. Soto. In that bureau I placed some
keepsakes, books, silver, my wedding dress and other articles I valued. Mrs· Soto begged me to send the bureau to
her in the night-time so that none of her neighbors should
know. These things she faithfully kept for me till we returned in September, 1847.

Our three children were sometimes in the wood cart and
sometimes in front of the riders—Agatha the baby in my
lap. Mrs. Elliott had a good large carryall, Mrs. Bradley
a fine wagon and some riding horses. Annie Bradley
rode on horseback with Mr. Maverick and myself. The
weather was charming, the grass green and the whole
earth in bloom—and I cannot forget the gay gallops we
had going ahead and resting 'til the others came up.
Strange that we refugees should be such a happy crowd,
but so it was. So it always will be with youth and health
—heedless of trouble and misfortune awaiting us.

The first day we travelled only five miles and camped
on the west bank of the Salado. It rained gently on us
that night and the children and I crept under our little
tent. Mr. Maverick was on guard part of the time, or
asleep in his blanket before the camp fire. Once it rained
so hard that he took refuge under Judge Hutchinson's
carriage, in which Mrs. Hutchinson was sleeping. While

he was lying there awake, Judge Hutchinson came up, opened the door, and remarking to Mrs. Hutchinson that he had just been relieved from guard and was wet and cold, was proceeding to enter the carriage, when Mrs. Hutchinson said in rather discouraging tones: "What makes you such a fool as to stand guard? You know you can't see ten feet." "Well, my love, can't I come in?" "No, my dear, you can't, you are damp and would give me a bad cold." The judge resignedly closed the door and retired to the camp-fire, where he smoked his pipe, ruminating over the cruelty of his young second wife, or possibly over his own unwisdom in mentioning the fact that he was wet before he had gotten fairly in.

March 2nd. We traveled eighteen miles to the Cibolo and four miles to Santa Clara and camped. Here Colonel Ben McCulloch, Mr. Miller and several other gentlemen met and camped with us—they had armed in haste and were going out to San Antonio to "meet the enemy." They were as witty and lively as could be and we all sat late around the camp fire enjoying their jokes and "yarns." A guard was kept all night and in the morning when McCulloch's party was about to leave us, Colonel McCulloch told the ladies that Indians had been seen lurking in the neighborhood, which was the reason they had given us their protecting presence during the night.

March 3rd, twelve miles to Flores' Rancho near Seguin, and here we met Major Erskine of the Capote Farm, who had come purposely to meet and conduct us to his place, in good old Virginia style. He was an old acquaintance and friend of Mr Bradley, and also knew Mr. Maverick. We proceeded one mile further to Seguin when we camped for the night. Crossing the Guadalupe, Mrs. Elliott's carriage turned over, breaking a shaft, but without injuring anyone.

March 4th, Mr. Maverick, my brothers and many others left us for San Antonio, and we went on twelve miles to Major Erskine's. We were many, but they crowded us all into their hospitable house, gave us a fine supper, and a fine breakfast, and although Mrs. Erskine was an invalid confined to her bed at the time, they extended to us the kindest attentions, and treated us all like kin.

March 5th, after breakfast we insisted on relieving the kind people and taking care of ourselves. Mrs. Elliott, Mrs. Jacques and I took possession of the blacksmith shop in the yard, and Mr. Gautier's family took a shed alongside the shop. The Bradleys remained housed with the Erskines, and the Hutchinsons went on east. We had great fun decorating our domicile. We placed flowers and green boughs in the chinks, and erected a shelf on which we placed a borrowed mirror, and our perfumery bottles and bric-a-brac, and we made ourselves at home generally. The servants stretched tents near by and cooked us a nice supper.

March 6th. Early, to-wit at three a. m., Captain Highsmith rapped loudly on our door and, when we had answered, called out in a solemn voice: "Ladies, San Antonio has fallen." It was startling news indeed, and the night being very dark and cold, we were seized with a vague sense of terror. Mrs Jacques lit a candle and commenced weeping bitterly. Mrs. Elliott fell on her knees and counted her beads oftener than once, and I took a shaking ague and could not speak for the chatter of my teeth. The children waked and cried, the negroes came in with sad and anxious looks, and we were in fact seized with a genuine "panic."

Then Mr. Gautier learned from Captain Highsmith that the Americans had fallen back in good order, with their cannon—that General Rafael Vasquez with a large force had entered San Antonio on the 5th, and that the Americans believing Vasquez' forces to be the vanguard of a large army, had decided upon making Seguin our rendezvous, and were gradually retreating to that point.* That miserable day, all day, rumors came, cour-

---

*On March 6, '42 Gen. Vasquez with 1400 Mexican troops appeared and captured San Antonio. No battle was fought and they retreated across the Rio Grande during the same month. This was the time when John Twohig blew up his store. G. M. Maverick.

iers passed in haste, and we were informed that an army of thirty thousand Mexicans had cut our forces up and was marching directly toward Capote Farm, presumably intending to cross the Guadalupe at this point.

During the excitement in the morning, Mrs. Jacques buried her money, and Mrs. Elliott constructed three bustles, for herself and her two servant-women, and in the bustles she deposited her gold doubloons, and we had all prepared and recited what we should say to the Mexican officers upon their arrival.   After dinner, we all went out to the public road and sat down on a log, all in a row and watched to see them approach, whilst the invalid Mr. Douglas, wearing his comical long red-silk smoking cap tried to cheer and amuse us with his jokes and witticisms. Soon towards the fatal west was seen an approaching horseman urging his tired steed with whip and spur—"A Courier!" cried Douglas, "Now we shall know all."   Sure enough it was my dear brother Andrew come to set us at ease about the personal safety of our absent husbands, as he had a better horse than they, for our husbands appreciated our anxiety, and had sent him forward as their avant courier, and before dark Mr. Maverick and Mr. Elliott came, followed soon afterwards by Mr. Bradley and Mr. Jacques.

Hays sent us word to go right on to Gonzales, and we were informed that he with some three hundred men had concluded to march on San Antonio and attempt its recapture, Hays having satisfied himself that no additional forces were sustaining Vasquez.   On March 9th, Hays with three hundred men entered San Antonio, and on his approach, Vasquez with eight hundred men fell back across the Rio Grande, after having done considerable damage to property in San Antonio.

Meanwhile we had gone to Gonzales, where Mr. Maverick left us again and returned to San Antonio. We remained in Gonzales until April 16th.   The Bradleys remained with the Erskines awhile and then went to the Brazos in company with the Chalmers.   At Gonzales,

Mrs. Riddle overtook us and joined me in the house I was occupying—a house vacated by the owners, who had fled further east. Mr. Robinson, partner of her husband, brought Mrs. Riddle from San Antonio in a buggy behind a fleet horse. She became very sick, and for a time could not nurse her baby, a little more than three weeks old, and I gave her little Sallie a portion of Agatha's milk until Mrs. Riddle recovered.

On the way from Capote farm to Gonzales, we had passed King's Rancho, which had just been deserted by the owners. Here was desolation amidst plenty. The corn crib was full, the smoke house well supplied and chickens and hogs moved around as usual—but on the front door a notice was posted: "To all refugees, welcome, help yourselves to what you need. Also, to all marching to repel the invaders, take what you want, but leave the remainder to the next comers." This at first appeared remarkable, but it was founded in wisdom. All along the Guadalupe and even the Colorado, families ran away from their homes in the same way, and great losses followed. My brothers William and Andrew, living on the San Marcos, sent their negroes each with a "run away" family, and went to the front with Caldwell and McCulloch, and while they were absent some wanton passersby left their fences down and their hogs were killed and stolen—their cattle strayed, and finally a flood came in May, swept away their bottom fences, and broke them up. Andrew left affairs with William, and in the summer went back to Alabama to complete his medical studies in Tuskaloosa, intending to return eventually with his diploma; he also had some property there from Mother's estate to attend to. While we were in Gonzales, I met Mr. and Mrs. Vanderlip, young people, living there, who afterwards came to San Antonio. Mrs. Vanderlip had a piano and was very pretty and not long from New York City. I met also Mrs. Ballinger of South Carolina and her sister Miss Roach, afterwards Mrs. Frank Paschal.

A singular panic occurred in Gonzales when we were

there. One evening an old and respected citizen came in
from the country northwest of town, and, in a state of the
greatest excitement reported that a large force of Indians
was enroute coming down the river direct for Gonzales
and would certainly arrive during the ensuing night. He
said they could easily take and destroy the town, weak-
ened in force as it was. This report spread swiftly and
created the wildest excitement. The people from the
suburbs and adjacent country crowded rapidly into the
central part of the town, and many came to our house, for
five or six gentlemen, well known as brave men, were to
be the defenders of our house in case of an attack. The
people came in pell-mell, they crowded into my room and
Mrs. Riddle's room, and there was no chance for sleep or
privacy that long night. They ate all the provisions we
had in the house, (tho' stored in a large fireplace and covered up,) the children cried, and we had a dreadful night
of it. The men stood guard, they barricaded the doors
and windows, they furnished us women with pistols and
knives and every hour or so they reported, "All's well."
Patrols and pickets took care of the various roads and al-
together everybody, except probably the old gentleman,
had a frightful night.

The old fellow who started all the hubbub became
sick apparently, and went off somewhere to sleep, and in
the morning they found that he had gone crazy from the
excitement of the times. His story had been a mere vagary
of his disordered mind, and no Indians were near us.

Mr. Maverick returned to us in April. He had found
our house robbed of everything. We had built a brick wall
and a walnut mantel-piece together, so as to divide our
"long-room" into two apartments, and even this mantel
had been forced out of the wall and carried off. It had
been sand-papered and oil-rubbed until it looked beautiful, and they took it for some rare wood. Mrs. Hutchinson's piano had been chopped open with an axe and all
kinds of damage had been done to anything belonging to
Americans.

Mr. Maverick found it necessary to make another trip to the United States, and, being desirous of leaving us in a perfectly safe place during his absence, he concluded to take us to the Colorado River near La Grange, and leave us there until his return.

April 16th, we set out for the Colorado, Andrew accompanying us, and travelled twelve miles to McClures.

A presentiment fulfilled. On April 17th, we travelled twenty-eight or thirty miles to Mr. Chadong's on the west bank of the Navidad. It was on this day's trip that I experienced a memorable foreboding which saved us from disaster. We had travelled about twenty-two miles when we reached a lone log house, where a family, O'Bar, I think, had been massacred by the Indians four years previously. This house was much used by travellers as a stopping place, and we had expected to stop there, and now it was dusk and very cloudy, and we had every reason to wish to remain there during the night, for it was eight miles to the next place; but as I rode up to the doorless cabin and looked into the large room, which appeared all right, a strange feeling of danger came over me so strongly that I turned and said to my husband and brother, "Don't think of staying here for something very dreadful will happen if you do." They laughed, and bantered me on being afraid of Indians, but I answered. "Not Indians, I don't know what it is, but we must go on."

We, people and beasts, were all very tired, but I was so urgent that we all went on after waiting for the cart a little while. Soon after, a tremendous thunder storm swept over us, the wind whistled mournfully, the lightning flashed vividly about us and the rain poured down in torrents. A tree at the roadside, just ahead of us, was torn to pieces by a lightning stroke. The road was full of water directly and our horses could only walk, so that it was after midnight when we approached Chadong's house. But our trouble was not ended then— a ravine crossed our path between us and the house and it was overflowing its banks. Andrew swam over and found a fair crossing, and then came back and led my horse. Agatha was sleeping in my arms at the time. I had kept her tolerably dry, and she slept peacefully through it all. Lewis was asleep in front of his papa and was kept dry by his Mexican blanket. After we had called repeatedly Mr. Chadong opened his door, and when he learnt who we were he apologized for keeping us out in the storm so long. He said he had to be cautious because of the dangerous times, and that it was not safe to let everybody in. He told us of a better crossing, and Andrew went back to guide the balance of our people over, and returned holding Sam in his arms.

The kind people of the house did all they could for us —they built big fires, spread beds for us on the floor, and the children were soon asleep again. I turned about, and dried my clothes upon me and did not sleep 'til near day, the hogs were so noisy under the house, and the fleas so thick within. On the 18th, and until the 20th, the Navidad was impassable, and so we moved into Mr. Chadong's corn crib and kept house for ourselves.

In the course of the day a man following our route informed us that the storm of the previous night had blown down the deserted log cabin which I had refused to enter, roof and big logs all in ruins lay scattered upon the ground. We were very thankful for our Divine guidance from this certain death to some of us, had we camped in the house.

Our travel of the day before had been uncommon to say the least. We crossed the "bald prairie" which Indians were believed to be always watching, and through which ran their trail, generally passed over by them in the full of the moon, to steal and often murder or take captives. We had a very early start and only stopped at mid-day to lunch, and to rest our animals—the cart was lightly loaded and the people preferred to walk much of the time— but in eighteen hours we had gone twenty-eight or thirty miles—and we were wet, hungry and tired dreadfully yet no one of us was sick, or even had a cold.

While we were living in the corn crib, Mrs. Chadong invited us to dine with her. She had young chickens and green peas, and tarts of Mustang grapes, sweetened with molasses, the only sweetening to be had. They had coffee without milk or cream, although they were large cattle owners. They were very kind and hospitable to us, and we enjoyed the excellent dinner and their good cheer very much.

April 20th, Andrew went back, and we crossed the Navidad and travelled eighteen miles to Buckner's Creek and stopped at Major Brookfield's—21st, six miles to the Colorado River.

On the west bank of the Colorado stood the office of Colonel J. W. Dancy, and the vacant house adjoining just left so by the family of Enoch Jones who had fled further east. Mr. Griff. Jones a brother was there and Mr. McAhron, the ferryman. They begged us to stop and take charge of the house, alleging that they were lonesome and were tired cooking for themselves. We rested there one week, and on the 29th, we returned to Brookfield's on Buckner's Creek, where we engaged board with his daughter, Mrs. Evans.

April 30th. Today Mr. Maverick left us to go to Alabama. He left to collect some money due him in Tuskaloosa and also for the purpose of bringing back with him my sister Elizabeth. None of my brothers were married, and as I was the only one who could offer her the comforts of a home, she had concluded to brave our wild country and unite her fortune with ours.

May 13th. Anton Lockmar rode expressly from San Antonio with letters from John Bradley and J. W. Smith, from which we learned that all Americans had left that place again—that seven hundred Mexicans were ten miles below and would probably seize the town, for our volunteers had disbanded and gone home. Radaz and some others were captured by the Mexicans thirty miles below San Antonio. About twenty men under Hays were out west and had overstaid their appointed time, and fears were entertained for their safety—Cornelius Van Ness had been accidently shot and killed by James Robinson.

May 23d. Agatha had burning fever for three hours. Dr. Wells gave her senna.

May 24th. News from LaGrange gave report that fifty Comanches had been seen on Peach Creek twenty miles from us. Most of the young men in that vicinity left in pursuit of the Indians.

May 26th. The young men returned, had found no fresh trail.

June 2nd. Heard of Major Tom Howard and Mr. Hudson passing through Columbus going west. They were in the Santa Fe expedition, had been taken prisoners and had escaped.

June 11th. Mr. Maverick returned from Alabama with my sister Lizzie . They came upon horseback from Galveston, via Mobile and New Orleans, having bought horses for themselves and a new saddle for me.

June 21st. We returned to General Dancy's, and took up our residence at his place, until we could provide a home for ourselves. This place is in Fayette County, opposite La Grange on the Colorado.

August 22nd. Mr. Maverick, with servant Griffin, J. Beale, Grif. Jones and Mr. Jackson set off for San Antonio to attend the Fall Term of Court. Griffin went along to bring back whatever he could find of our furniture. Lizzie and I and Colonel Dancy accompanied them six or seven miles of their way. I felt much depressed at saying goodbye, and deplored the necessity of his going so much, that Mr. Maverick remarked: "Almost you persuade me not to go."

Alas! too surely and swiftly came a terrible sorrow.

MISSION SAN JOSE (Second Mission)

Chapter XI.

PEROTE.

September 11th, Sunday morning, at day-break, General Adrian Woll with a large force of Mexicans consisting of cavalry and artillery to the number of thirteen hundred suddenly appeared before San Antonio, and captured the place. It was a complete surprise. The court was in session at the time, and, including the members of the bar and Judge of the district Court, fifty-three Americans were captured, one of whom was Mr. Maverick.

Before the little band surrendered, they showed a bold and vigorous front, even in the face of such fearful odds. They fortified themselves in the Maverick residence at the corner of Commerce and Soledad Streets—some of them mounted upon the roof, when Mr. John Twohig received a wound from which he has never entirely recovered. When the Mexican troops entered Main Plaza, the Texans fired upon them briskly, killing two and wounding twenty-six, six of whom died of the wounds.

General Woll beat a parley, and after he had shown the Texans they could not escape him and had promised to treat them as honorable prisoners of war and used some other plausible talk with them, the Texans held a consultation among themselves, when a majority voted to surrender. After they surrendered, they were kept in the Maverick residence, where they were closely guarded until the 15th.

Mrs. Elliott was in San Antonio when my husband was captured, and she was allowed to visit the prisoners once or twice before they were taken off to Mexico. Mr. Maverick found an opportunity to hand Mrs. Elliott twenty gold doubloons for me.

No one can imagine how dreadful this news was to me, especially when I learned that our poor prisoners were marched off on foot for Mexico on 15th. At this time my poor little Lewis was dangerously ill with fever then prevalent in the neighborhood. Our slave Griffin had come back from San Antonio and was greatly troubled about his master, to whom he was much attached. I called him to me, and talked to him about going out to San Antonio to pass himself for a runaway, follow to Mexico, and do anything he could to free or even aid Mr. Maverick, and he could have his freedom. He answered that to do anything for his master would delight him, and he had been wanting to ask me to let him go—"as for my freedoom," he added, "I do not want any more than I have, master has always treated me more like a brother than a slave," and he choked up unable to say more. He took a gun, a good mule, some money, and made ready and started within a few hours—happy to think he might do something to help his master. 15th, Juan Seguin killed Dr. Smithers, McDonald and McRhea at the Sulphur Springs on the Cibolo. 17th, 163 men under Mat Caldwell are on the Cibolo going west. 18th, Caldwell moved with 225 men to the Salado, and on the morning of the 19th, selecting a ravine for his force, he ordered Hays with 50 mounted men to draw the Mexicans out of San Antonio.

The Battle of the Salado. This battle ground was on the left bank of the Salado about six miles from San Antonio and a mile below the Austin crossing of that creek. Hays maneuvered to success, and feigning flight, was hotly pursued by the two hundred Mexican cavalry to the Salado, who then halted and awaited the arrival of the main body of one thousand infantry (dismounted men) and a battery of two guns.

My brothers William and Andrew were both with Caldwell, and they afterwards told me all about the battle. The Mexicans charged in style. The Texans held their fire until they "could see the whites of the eyes" of their foes—then each "picked his man and laid him low," and the Mexicans were repulsed with considerable slaughter. They returned to the charge again and again, but were repulsed each time with great loss. The battle lasted from eleven o'clock, a. m. until five in the afternoon, when the the Mexicans were repulsed with considerable slaughter. back on San Antonio. General Woll reported his loss as one hundred killed, but our people claimed three times as many. Amongst the Mexicans slain were Agaton and Cordova, two famous leaders of marauding parties. Not a Texan was killed and only ten were wounded. My brothers told me it was a pleasure to our boys to shoot down those Mexicans, "for they had broken up all our homes and taken many of our brave comrades into cruel captivity."

On the morning of the battle, the Texans had butchered some beeves, but before they could get their breakfast, the order was given to fall in. But after the fight commenced, and they found it was such an easy going affair, after each charge was repulsed, and before the Mexicans slowly reformed and advanced again, our boys would descend into the ravine and take a lunch of broiled meat and hot coffee. They joked and sang and were very gay, and they wanted nothing better than to have the Mexicans come up and be shot—it seemed like child's play. They themselves were quite secure behind the banks of the ravine and the cannon balls passed above and over them.

The Dawson Massacre. During the day of the battle of the Salado, Captain Dawson with his brave fifty-nine men from Fayette County, seeking a junction with the main force under Caldwell met a bloody and cruel fate. They fell in with Woll's army and were surrounded by eight hundred Mexican troops when within one mile of Caldwell. Our faithful Griffin was with Dawson's company. They fought so desperately that the Mexicans brought their two cannon to bear upon them, when Dawson, seeing there was no hope of escape, raised the "white flag." This was fired upon, and the Mexican cavalry, disregarding the surrender, charged upon the gallant remnant and cut them down on every side. It was then that Dawson was slain. Colonel Carasco interfered at this moment and fifteen Texans were taken prisoners—three or four of whom died of their wounds. Thirty-three had been slain and the rest escaped.*

Mr. Miller escaped on a fine horse before the white flag was raised. My uncle, Mr. John Bradley, was one of the prisoners. Ten of them, including Mr. Bradley, were marched off to Mexico, and finally joined the fifty-three who had started on the 13th.

Our poor Griffin was slain. He would go into the fight with them and though offered quarter several times refused because he was thinking of his master, now a prisonerer, and too, of his young masters, William and Andrew, now possibly slain; the desire for vengeance seized his brave and trusty soul, and he wanted to kill every Mexican he could. He was a man of powerful frame, and he posessed the courage of the African lion. And this faithful and devoted African performed prodigies that day. When his ammunition became useless because of the proximity of the enemy, he fought with the butt-end of his gun and when the gun was broken, he wrenched a limb from a mesquite-tree and did battle with that until death closed his career. He received more than one mortal wound before he ceased fighting.*

The Mexican Colonel Carasco himself afterwards told Mr. Maverick that he had witnessed the feats performed by "that valiant black man," and he pronounced Griffin the bravest man he had ever seen. Mr. Maverick grieved over his untimely death, and more than once did he say: "We owe Griffin a monument."

September 20th. The Mexican citizens of San Antonio who espoused the Mexican cause, with a guard of four

---

*Thrall says the battle took place on the 17th. He says that as Gen. Woll retreated he fell in with Dawson's company of 55 men—33 were slain, 15 surrendered and 2 escaped (he doesn't account for the other five men). He says Woll retreated the following morning from S. A. and that a misunderstanding as to who was entitled to command prevented pursuit by the Texans.

*Brown's history says "Griffin" was killed with Dawson. G. M. M.

SAN JUAN OR THIRD MISSION

MISSION SAN FRANCISCO DE LA ESPADA, OR 4th MISSION

hundred soldiers, left San Antonio for Mexico, taking with them five hundred head of cattle and much plunder.

September 21st, General Woll, with his remaining forces evacuated San Antonio, and retired in good order towards the Rio Grande. Colonel Caldwell with six hundred and fifty men pursued them, and at night came upon their camp on the Medina. At daylight the next morning, the Texans found the enemy had retreated during the night—they gave chase, and caught up with them early in the afternoon. Caldwell ("Old Paint") commanded the first division, Morehead the second and John H. Moore the third or reserve. J. H. Moore was the ranking officer, but Caldwell immediately took active command, and prepared for the battle. He commanded Hays with twenty picked men to make a diversion on the enemy's left. Hays, with his usual dash and gallantry, entered vigorously into the spirit of the hour. He charged boldly into the ranks of the enemy and immediately captured the artillery. The Mexicans threw their women and children into the space between the captured artillery and their main army. Then came a dreadful pause. A disgraceful scene was being enacted in the Texan army. J. H. Moore claimed his right as ranking officer to conduct the battle. Caldwell's men refused to be commanded by anyone other than the hero of the Salado. Morehead's men demanded that Morehead should command. After some delay Caldwell awoke to the importance of action and announced that he would follow Moore or any other man, and take all his men into the fight with him. But the contention had lasted too long; the important moment had come and had fled forever. Hays' small band had captured the artillery, and the enemy was already casting timorous glances toward the rear—a charge by the Texans would have scattered them to the winds. As it was, Hays was in a perilous position—the enemy had time to recover from the first shock—they charged upon Hays in force and drove him from the field. Hays fell back out of range and witnessed Woll's army successfully retire from the field and resume the march westward. Hays' gallant

spirit was wounded by this unaccountable and ignomini-
ous scene and his feelings found utterance in tears—yes,
tears of shame and rage. The Texan army at last came
forward, but it was too late, the enemy had escaped. The
Texans were so disgusted and mortified that all discipline
was lost and they returned in angry and humiliated
squads to San Antonio. Hays had five wounded in his
brilliant encounter, one of whom, Judge Lucky, died.
The Mexicans abandoned their extra baggage and fled
precipitately across the Rio Grande.

The blame of the failure was cast principally upon
Colonel Caldwell, and he felt so humiliated and outraged
that he became restive under the heavy burden and from
a condition of excellent health, he sank into despondency
and died of chagrin two or three months later. But his
memory remained fresh and revered. He had been a
noted Indian fighter, as I have mentioned before, and he
had been an officer in the unfortunate Santa Fe expedition, and had suffered imprisonment. He had a great and
good reputation throughout west Texas.

I now return to Mr. Maverick, and other prisoners
captured on September 11th, in San Antonio during the
Term of the Court.

On March 30th, 1843, Mr. Maverick, W. E. Jones and
Judge Anderson Hutchinson were finally released in the
City of Mexico by Santa Anna. Our obligations to General Waddy Thompson can never be forgotten. General
Thompson was a native of South Carolina, and a connection by marriage of Mr. Maverick's. He was the United
States Minister to Mexico. After securing the release of
Mr. Maverick, Jones and Hutchinson, he nobly exerted
his influence to secure the release of all the other helpless
and friendless prisoners, and he did not cease his efforts
until he had succeeded in getting them all—all the survivors—liberated.

On April 2nd, 1843, Mr. Maverick, once more free,
left the City of Mexico, and on May 4th, he dismounted
at our cabin on the Colorado, having been absent from

his family eight and a half months, and a prisoner seven months.

Mr. Maverick's only sorrow was that he had left so many friends and comrades in prison, and he felt almost ashamed when he met any of their families and friends, who all, of course, came to see him—to tell them of his own good luck and of the continued ill luck of the other captives.

June 16th, 1843, Santa Anna, as a special favor to General Waddy Thompson, signed the release for the balance of the Perote prisoners, but the order for release was so slowly carried into execution that it was more than two months before Mr. Bradley reached his family.

Chapter XII.

COLORADO BOTTOMS.

E lived on the Colorado from June 21st, 1842, until November 15th, 1844. I have mentioned our arrival, June 21st, at Colonel Dancy's where we were to remain awhile. On August 21st, Mr. Maverick bought twenty-six acres of land, fronting on the right bank of the Colorado, and lying between two tracts belonging to Colonel Dancy. He had it surveyed by Hudson, and made arrangements to build us a temprorary home on it. This tract was opposite La Grange in Fayette County and opposite the ferry.

It was on August 22nd, as I have mentioned, that Mr. Maverick left us for San Antonio, where he was captured and taken to Perote. During September, poor little Lewis became ill with typhoid fever. Griffin came back about this time and returned on his fateful errand.

September 29th, I received a letter from my dear husband, now a captive. The letter was written on the eve of their being marched off to a Mexican dungeon. It was calm, cheerful and hopeful, and counseled me to be brave, to bear a stout heart, and to take care of myself and the children.

November 16th, we moved into our own house, which consisted of a log cabin of one room sixteen by eighteen feet, one smaller for a kitchen, and a shed room for Jinny and the children. This house was built by Granville and Wiley with much help from Mr. Griff. Jones, who was very kind to us. Lewis was now almost strong again. The fever had been severe with him, and had so reduced him, that he was unable to stand up for some time after it had left him.

My aunt, Mrs. Bradley, whose husband was also a prisoner in Perote, came to the Colorado and moved into Colonel Dancy's house, which I had just vacated. She and I had some sad consolation conferring together over our troubles, and comparing such news as each of us occasionally received from our imprisoned husbands or from Dame Rumor. Annie Bradley had gone to Alabama to visit her relatives. Mollie Bradley, my sister Lizzie, and Leonora Hill, daughter of a neighbor, became intimate companions, rode much on horseback together, and kept some youthful company and cheer of life about us.

In La Grange lived Dr. Chalmers' family, refugees from Austin. Here we met Thomas J. Devine, a young lawyer, and the Misses Elder, one of whom Devine married. We also met George Hancock and Tom Green.

As I have said Mrs. Elliott was in San Antonio when Mr. Maverick was captured. She visited the prisoners by permission, and Mr. Maverick handed her privately twenty gold doubloons for me, about $325.00 in our money. And the money came safely to me through John W. Smith. This amount with what I had in the house I tried to make go as far as possible. Coffee, sugar, and flour were very high, as indeed everything except beef, corn, fowls and butter. I had the twenty-six acre tract fenced in and purchased some milch cows.

My brother William came to see how I was doing, and stopped awhile with us, and worked with our men, until they built another log cabin, adjacent to the one previously built, leaving a passage or hall between them. In this hall we usually sat when the weather was fair. We had an immense live-oak tree for shade, and immediately in front of the house stood a "mott" of young live oak trees. In fact, we made ourselves as comfortable as possible under the circumstances. William remained with us as long as he could, and then left for Alabama.

In November I received a letter from my husband, written October 16th, at Monclova (Montelovez) Coahuila. He had marched four hundred miles and had eight hundred more, as he understood, to march before reaching the City of Mexico, where he expected to be released. My dear husband wrote to cheer me expressly, for he spoke of his excellent health, and hopefulness, but did not mention anything about the pens they were herded in at night, nor of the other abuses they were subjected to.

I, however, was constantly fearing that the next mail would bring some dreadful news from the prisoners—and only when I got an occasional letter so brave and fond, from S. A. M. could I hope. I tried to follow his advice, and kept up at times a semblance of cheerfulness, but I was then only twenty-four years of age, and almost a child in experience and I had the care of three helpless little children and the birth of a fourth to look to in the future. A refugee in a strange land and my husband a captive in the power of a cruel and treacherous foe. Ah, then I felt—"What weight of agony the human heart can bear." But I strove to be brave and prayed to God that I might live for my children and my dear husband.

In February, 1843, I received a letter from Mr. Maverick written January 27th, at Perote. He mentioned in it how badly they had been treated in Satillo—"that robber city of thirty thousand people, where we were closely confined in a filthy prison for fifteen days"—and where their captors threatened to take them to some secret place where they would never be heard from again. But in this letter, Mr. Maverick was quite hopeful of being released through the exertions of General Waddy Thompson, then United States Minister to Mexico.

This letter, full of deep feeling, along with other letters written by Mr. Maverick, whilst a prisoner, I have carefully preserved for our children as sacred. I have another written December 30th, 1842; one written February 2nd, 1843, also expecting speedy release. Another written March 15th, contains the same hope. March 22nd, he wrote again stating that he and W. E. Jones and Judge Anderson Hutchinson were released from prison. Their final release would be received in the City of Mexico. He wrote of Dr. Borken, one of "our San Antonio boys," being shot by a drunken soldier, and told of his dying in great bodily pain and mental agony, and he mentioned the death of General Guadalupe Victoria, the first President of the Republic of Mexico.

March 30th, 1843, on Thursday morning our second daughter was born—child of a captive father, and for him named Augusta. On the day of her birth, her father was finally released by Santa Anna in the City of Mexico. Mr. Maverick set out for home on the 2nd of April, and finally reached our cabin the night of May 4th, in splendid health, and happy as he could be and so was I, and thankful to our Heavenly Father for all His mercies. Augusta was five weeks old when she and her father met.

In June, Ada Bradley was born. In June and again September, Mr. Maverick visited San Antonio—to attend court and land business.

on the Brazos, the capital of the Republic of Texas, and

In December, 1843, Mr Maverick went to Washington attended the session of the Eighth Congress of the Republic, as Senator from Bexar. He had been elected whilst in Perote prison. He returned from Washington to spend Christmas with us at home, and we, with others, took Christmas dinner with the family of Dr. Chalmers in La-Grange.

1844.

The Congress adjourned on February 8th, 1844, and that was the last session of the last Congress of the Republic of Texas. Mr. Maverick soon after left for San Antonio, where he attended the March term of the District Court, and returned to us in April, and then started off on a visit to South Carolina.

Remarkable Indian Fight. On June 20th, 1844, Major Jack Hays came to see me and gave me the particulars of a noted encounter he had had with the Indians only twelve days before he called on me. The fight took place on June 8th. Hays, with fourteen men, was scouting on the Guadalupe about fifty miles above Seguin, (it must have been between the present sites of Sisterdale and Comfort in Kendall County). Whilst some of the Rangers were cutting a bee tree, the spies galloped up with the news that a very large party of Comanches were close upon them. At once the Rangers mounted and made ready—by this time the Indians had formed in admirable order on the level top of a hill near by. The Rangers following their leader, spurred forward in full charge, and, when they reached the foot of the hill which was steep and somewhat overhanging, they found they were no longer in sight of the enemy. Taking advantage of this, Hays led his men half around the base of the hill, still out of sight, and dashed up at a point not expected. The Comanches had dismounted, and were kneeling down with guns and arrows fixed for a deadly aim. Strange to say, Hays was close upon them before they discovered his stratagem, and before they could mount their horses, the Rangers were in their midst—shooting them right and left, with their new revolving pistols. But the Indians were numerous, some sixty-five or seventy warriors, and were led by two especially brave and daring chiefs. The chiefs rallied their forces and closed completely around the Rangers and fought with great daring, but the astonishing "six-shooters" did the work—the Indians speedily became demoralized and they broke and fled, leaving twenty-three of their comrades dead on the battle-field This was opportune, for the loads were exhausted in the six-shooters of the Rangers, and they immediately took advantage of the enemy's flight to reload their vigorous little weapons. The Indians, finding they were not pursued, paused and reformed for battle. The Rangers charged now with the same result. The fight lasted nearly an hour, the Indians fighting stubbornly and retiring slowly and still forty strong· A chief then made a great talk to his followers, rising in his stirrups and gesticulating—he rode up and down their lines and got them to make another desperate stand.

SAMUEL AUGUSTUS MAVERICK

The Rangers were reduced now to eleven fighting men, and Hays called out: "Any man who has a load, kill that chief." Ad Gillespie answered: "I'll do it," dismounted, aimed carefully with his trusty yager, and shot the chief dead, when a panic seized the Indians, and they fled in the utmost confusion.

Peter Fohr was killed, and four of the Rangers wounded and many arrows passed through their hats and clothing, for several thousand arrows were fired into their midst.

I wrote the memorandum of the fight just after Major Hays had related it. I was much struck with the odds in the numbers of the opposing forces,—fifteen against sixty-five or seventy, and with Hays' remark that "more than thirty Indians were killed."

Hays modestly gave the credit of the victory to the wonderful marksmanship of every Ranger, and the total surprise to the Indians, caused by the new six shooters, which they had never seen or heard of before.

I quote Colonel Hays' closing remarks:

"We were right glad they fled, for we were nearly used up with the fatigue of a long day's march that day and the exertions on the battle-field, and we were almost out of ammunition. The Indians made a magnificent fight under the circumstances. They seemed to be a band of selected braves in full war-paint, and were led by several chiefs, showing that they were marching down upon the settlements, where they would have devided into parties commanded each by a chief, and great would have been the mischief done by such a number of savages."

August 11th, our dear little Agatha came near being killed. Brother Andrew came to see us on his way to Alabama, and, dismounting, hitched his gentle horse under the shade of the large live oak tree. Some time afterwards, Agatha was playing near the horse's heels when the horse, kicking at a fly, struck her on the forehead and buried a small piece of his hoof in her head. She screamed and fell down and when her father picked her up she was in convulsions. We picked the scrap of hoof out of her forehead, bathed her head in cold water and we sat almost hopeless at her side awaiting the result. At midnight she became quiet and went to sleep, and just before daybreak she opened her eyes and said: "Papa, give me a drink of water." He said with deep emotion: "Blessed be God," and she was out of danger. Under the doctor's advice, we took great care of her, and kept her out of the sun for some time.

In the summer of 1843, the balance of the Perote prisoners received their liberation, and Mr. Bradley soon thereafter reached his family. In the summer of 1844, Mr. Bradley was persuaded to run for Congress. Whilst out electioneering, he was taken down with a fever, of which he died September 24th. Pauline Bradley was also quite ill at this time. Annie had married Robert Bibb, of Alabama, and they came out to see Aunt Ann directly after Mr. Bradley's death. When Mrs. Bibb returned to Alabama, Mrs. Bradley with her children took her negroes and moved out to San Antonio. Mrs. Bradley was self reliant, and she determined to provide for the large family left in her widowed care. How ably and successfully she performed that difficult task is quite well known.

For some weeks after her accident, Agatha was quite pale and she had a long and severe chill about the first of September. The doctor gave her quinine and she was soon a perfect picture of rosy health. Sam had a spell of chills and fever, and I became at last quite sickly myself during the summer. In fact, I became much reduced and was an invalid all the fall.

We concluded it would not do to live here any longer; the Colorado bottoms were too unhealthy. Mr. Maverick decided to take us to the Gulf Coast where we could enjoy sea bathing.

Chapter XIII.

LIFE ON THE PENINSULA.

THE Pass, or waterway, which connects Matagorda Bay with the Gulf of Mexico, is bounded on the south by Matagorda Island, the northern extremity of which is named Saluria, and on the north by Decrows Point, which is the southwestern extremity of the Peninsula. The pass is called Paso Caballo, and it is about three miles from Decrows Point to Saluria.

The Peninsula extends northeastwardly from Decrows Point, a distance of about fifty miles to the main land. Where the Peninsula joins the main land, Caney Creek formerly emptied into the Gulf of Mexico, but the creek has been diverted by means of a canal and now empties its scanty waters into the northern arm of Matagorda Bay. The Peninsula is a dreary, sandy flat, having an average width of about two miles; at the middle of this elongated strip of land is Tiltona, which was our farm. We lived at Decrows Point from December 7th, 1844, until October 15th, 1847, when we returned to San Antonio.

On November 15th, 1844, we deserted our temporary home on the Colorado, and set out for Decrows Point. We had a carriage and two hired wagons, some saddle horses and seven cows. I was an invalid during the whole trip, and travelled lying down in the carriage. A wide board was laid from the front to the back seat of the large roomy carriage, and quilts and pillows were bestowed where they would give me the most comfort. The driver's seat was on the outside. My dear little girls were generally with me, and sometimes Lizzie, but she usually preferred to ride on horseback with Mr. Maverick. Sam and Lewis rode in a wagon. We spent the first night in LaGrange at Mrs. Angus McNeil's, a third or fourth cousin of mine.

16th, got started in the afternoon and travelled only a few miles and camped. It rained and stormed all that night, and the next morning we started off in a norther.

17th, five miles to Rutersville. Mrs. Butler took us in, and she and Mrs. Robb were very kind. We established ourselves in a vacant house and waited for the weather to moderate.

November 21st, twelve miles to Breedings.

November 22nd, eight miles to Ohmburg's; 23rd, eighteen miles to Alley's; 24th, sixteen miles to Major Montgomery's; 25th, eighteen miles to Crawford's (Spanish Springs), 26th, sixteen miles to Cayce's; 27th, six miles to Dawson's (wiggle-tail mud pond, awfully dirty water); 28th, six miles to Captain John Duncan's; took dinner, and six miles to Mrs. Hardeman's, where we spent the night; 29th, six miles to Rindrick's, kindest people of all; took dinner here, and eight miles to Shepherd's, which is two miles into the swamps; 30th, awful roads, swamps continuously, crossed three sloughs, in the last one of which Granville's wagon stalled and one ox fell. He beat the ox awfully, and then they prized him out and doubled teams and got through. Made eight miles today and camped. In the night it rained and a norther blew up, and we all got cold and wet.

December 1st, Sunday, five miles to the new canal, crossed it with great difficulty, and camped. 2nd, half a mile to a vacant house, where we camped. 3rd, one mile, came to Gulf of Mexico—magnificent, calm, gently heaving water, and fourteen miles on the beautiful, smooth, hard beach, where we saw many bright shells. 4th, six miles to Mrs. Love's, where we took dinner, and five miles to Sergeant's and camped. Mrs. Sergeant gave us fresh butter-milk and butter and some coffee. 5th, seven miles in an awful north wind and rain, but we all lived through it, and camped in a shanty. 6th, eighteen miles and we camped on the beach. It was cold and the smoke of the camp fire intolerable. I lost all admiration for the "deep and dark blue ocean," and was most miserable and sick.

On December 7th, we travelled seven miles to Decrows Point—still in a brisk norther, but delighted to arrive at our journey's end, and have rest once more. We moved into a house occupied by Judge and General Somerville, the arrangement being that we should keep house and furnish them board, they to retain a portion of the house. General Somerville was the Revenue Officer for the Port—collector of revenue. The house was very close to the bay, and every evening Mr. Maverick took me down to bathe in the salt water.

December 12th. Had the pleasure of an introduction to His Highness Charles Solm Solm, son of the Grand Duke of Braunfels, and who was on his way to the Colony of New Braunfels of which he was the founder. The Prince and suite spent a day and night with us, and the Somervilles. Next evening he came near to land in his vessel and serenaded us.

General Somerville was a noted laugher—he saw the Prince's two attendants dress his Highness, that is lift him into his pants, and General Somerville was so overcome by the sight that he broke out into one of his famous fits of laughter, and was heard all over the Point. The Prince and suite were all very courteous and polite to us. They wore cock feathers in their hats, and did not appear quite fitted to frontier life.

1845.

We had a block of ground fenced in, and early in 1845 we planted a garden. It was wonderful how every thing grew, and what fine vegetables we had and what delicious watermelons! Flowers, grapevines and orange trees flourished luxuriantly.

In March, Agatha's clothes caught on fire, but Jack

threw a bucket of water on her and put the fire out, before she was badly burned. She was quite sore for several weeks afterwards.

June 11th, Mr. Maverick visited San Antonio, and was gone six weeks. On his return he took a sail boat at Lavaca, and before they had gotten out of sight of Lavaca a sudden squall capsized the boat, and he with several other passengers came very near being drowned—but being still near enough to Lavaca to be seen with the spyglass, they were observed and a small boat put out immediately, and rescued them just before dark. I am told by Mr. Dawson, now in Mr. Grenet's store, in San Antonio, that he was one of the rescuing party.

During this month, Mary McNeil came to see us. She and her uncle, Henry McNeil, were on their way to her mother's old home in Mississippi, where Mary was to attend school.

One afternoon the McNeils with General Somerville, Lizzie, Mr. Maverick and myself and Sam and Lewis went sailing on the bay, as we frequently did for pleasure, or to fish. or to gather gulls' eggs on the islets. The day was beautiful and we sailed seven or eight miles when we noticed a fog gathering, and, since we had not a pilot as we usually had aboard, we hastened to tack about and return, with General Somerville, a pretty good sailor, at the helm. But the fog came on so rapidly, and grew so dense that we could not see ten yards beyond the boat, and were soon satisfied that we were lost. We tacked, and we tacked, and we tacked again, but to no avail, we couldn't find our way out—and we were right glad when, about ten o'clock that night, we ran well aground. We remained there safely until daylight. We ladies were much alarmed, besides being damp, cold and hungry, and we at last crowded into a diminutive cabin to avoid a drizzling rain which now set in. Sam and Lewis were gotten to sleep quite early. The gentlemen hauled in the sails and made bed covers with them and went to sleep. Lizzie and Mary also slept, but I lay awake all night listening to the wash of the waves, and the roar of the breakers at the Pass, and I hailed with delight the dawn of day. General Somerville declared we were twelve miles from home, on the mainland on the west side of the bay. The gentlemen got out into the water, pushed the boat off, and it was still early morning when we hove to and greeted the anxious faces of our friends. Some of the people at the Point feared we were drowned, others blew fog horns and built big fires on the coast and kept them burning all night, but we had neither heard nor seen anything. We were all thankful to get safely back and put on dry clothing, and we attacked the warm breakfast with great gusto. I was delighted to see Agatha and Augusta, and I was told the poor little things had cried themselves to sleep the night before. No one suffered any harm from the exposure, and our experience of the night gave us many hearty laughs thereafter.

July, 1845. Thank God, we are now annexed to the United States, and can hope for home and quiet. Mr. Smith, American Consul in Saluria, was drowned in a bayou which he was attempting to cross, and his poor wife, an amiable, nice lady, left desolate and alone. We went over to see her, and Lizzie and Cora Vandever spent some time with her.

August 13th. Our family took quite an excursion up the bay. Went up Lavaca bay and landed opposite Lavaca at Tres Palacios (Cox's Point), where Mr. Maverick had long since purchased an interest in the land, as I have mentioned in Chapter III. This we found a beautiful site. Twenty Matagordians were here for the bathing, and we spent a few days at Captain Grimes's. Dr. Farquehar had a nice residence here and a garden of pretty flowers and rare plants and fruits.

We rented a house opposite the Levy's, and in the same block with the family of Mr. Forrester, who had been a Perote prisoner with Mr. Maverick. At that time, Matagorda had probably the most cultivated society in the state. Matagorda then had good schools, several

churches, and many well-to-do people, who had planta-
tions on the Caney and Colorado, where the summers
were quite unhealthful, had their summer residences
here.   Reverend Caleb Ives was the Episcopal Minister.
His wife, when she was Miss Kenneer, had been my teach-
er in Tuskaloosa.   They had charge of the academy for
young ladies in Matagorda.

On Sunday, September 7th, 1845, at seven p. m., our
fifth child, George Madison, was born.

August first, Miss Annie, daughter of Rhodes Fisher,
was married to Mr. J. W. Dallam.   Mr. Maverick and
Lizzie went to the wedding, and to several parties given
to the married couple by friends in Matagorda.

October 25th, we all returned by Schooner "Mary" to
Decrows Point, and had a house to ourselves.

October 28th, Mr. Maverick and Lizzie left by Schooner
"Mary" for New Orleans—Lizzie to Tuskaloosa for the
winter, and Mr. Maverick on business.

1846.

The 19th, January, we had a tempest.

January 28th, Mr. Lucius W. Peck came out, on Mr.
Maverick's advice, to teach school.   He came to our house,
sent hither by Mr. Maverick whom Mr. Peck had left
quite well in New Orleans.

March 17th, Mr. Maverick returned after an absence
of nearly five months.   He took Lizzie to Tuskaloosa
and remained there several weeks on business.   Thence
he went to Pendleton, where he visited Father Maverick,
and he found it "cruel to leave him in his precarious
health."   He remained with his father two weeks, and
received "his last sad embrace and blessing."   From
Pendleton he went to Charleston, where he was detained
by vexatious business one month.   At Charleston he
bought four negroes—viz: Frances and her boy Simon,
Naoma, a seamstress, and William, a carpenter.   He
wanted the carpenter because he had bought a one-third
interest in Decrows Point and intended to erect some

MARKET ON MILITARY PLAZA FROM PAINTING BY R. J. ONDERDONK,
OWNED BY MRS. ERHARD GUENTHER

houses. This purchase of negroes in Charleston soon proved to be a perfectly worthless investment. When Mr. Maverick reached New Orleans, he chartered a schooner, which he loaded with lumber for the improvements he intended to make at the Point, and on February 4th, he found it necessary to go to Mobile to complete his purchases. On March 9th, he left Mobile for Decrows Point on the chartered schooner, "Urbana," Captain Small. On board he had the negroes and the lumber and some goods and provisions. They had a stormy passage and narrow escape from going down during a gale. They entered Matagorda Bay, March 17th, happy to be with us again and gladly welcomed. Lewis cut a big "L" in one of the new chairs with his new knife first thing. Mr. Peck taught Sam and Lewis regularly at this time.

Dr. Gray Jones Houston and his brother Ross visited Texas during the winter of 1845-6. They came to see us in March 1846, and spent a few days with us. Mr. Maverick was in New Orleans at the time. It was about the 15th, when the north wind blew almost a gale and the bay rose very high, and the water of the bay seemed higher than the land, as it was driven southward through the Pass. The Houstons had decided to remove with their families and worldly goods from Alabama to Texas, but Dr. Houston said he would not settle on the Peninsula, at any rate, for he considered life quite unsafe here.

March 18th. The "Petrel" wrecked with two hundred German immigrants aboard. All lives saved by Captain Simptorn of the revenue cutter "Alert." Mrs. Neil, of San Antonio, was aboard. About this time, I learned of the marriage of my brother William to L. A. Goodman, in Freestone County at Troy on the Trinity River. There he was established as a merchant. My brother George M. Adams died April 26th, 1846, in Aberdeen, Mississippi, of congestive chills. He was twenty-eight years of age. He was an affectionate, good brother and a courageous man.

In June and July, we were gladdened by the news of

the two brilliant victories gained by General Taylor at Palo Alto and Resaca de la Palma.

In June, Lewis, Agatha and Augusta had the whooping cough. In September, every one of the children had the measles—Lewis was quite sick, and George had sore ears afterwards. Augusta was packed in a wet sheet to compel the measles to the surface. During September, the smallpox being prevalent, the children were all vaccinated and all took well. In October, Mrs. Maggie Peareson (nee Shortridge) spent some time at the Pass for her little girl's health. They were living at that time in Victoria. She boarded at Mrs. Vandever's across the street from us. We were great friends and spent many hours together. Parties from the country often came to the Pass, to fish and bathe and get away from mosquitoes, for we had none, and were always cool.

November 11th, Mr. Maverick visited San Antonio. He wrote of Charley Bradley's death of measles, and he stated there was much sickness in town, probably aggravated by the fevers and dysenteries of the soldiers in the camps, and by the continued ill health of the German immigrants, and that many deaths had occurred. In December Mr. Maverick bought the Nixon house and two lots.

1847.

January 3d, 1847, Mr. Maverick returned from San Antonio. I had heard many rumors of Indians on the road, and had suffered much uneasiness.

February 18th, Lizzie and Andrew arrived from Tuskaloosa. Lizzie had grown much improved and was fine looking and fashionably dressed. Andrew had his diploma with him and was now a regular M. D. The next day after his arrival, Andrew started for his old place on the San Marcos.

Purchase of Tiltona. March 16th, Mr. Maverick went to Tilton's place, twenty-five miles up the Peninsula, and bought it and four hundred head of cattle at $3.00 per head.* The place had an oyster bayou belonging to it

---

*See story and letters at end of book.

and pens for cattle, and there was a field in cultivation and some fine fig trees on the grounds.

March 19th, Friday, in the afternoon, Mr. Maverick was going up the stairway in the new house he was building for our residence, when he tripped on a loose step and fell twelve feet on the ground—striking on his shoulder. He was picked up insensible and brought in, his shoulder sprained terribly and neck twisted. When revived, he suffered agony for hours. We gave him twenty drops of laudanum and bathed the breast and shoulder with hot brandy and laudanum. We then also rubbed the bruised shoulder with mustard and placed hot bricks at his feet. He could not move, but felt some relief during the night and slept a little. After that he had fever and we used wet bandages. On the 21st, he could move his head and shoulder and became cheerful and his appetite returned. He was fed from a spoon, and he gradually gained strength—we had to rub the bruised place often and much, which seem to soothe the pain. Not until April 7th, was he able to get up and walk.

March 25th, Mr. McFee was upset in a small boat up the bay and his body was picked up at Indian Point.

April 1st—bright and warm—planted many garden seeds.

April 2nd, Jinny and Jack with Jane, Harriet and Laura went to Tiltona to take charge of the place. Wiley and Rachael and Rachael's child had some time previously been conveyed to Mr. Decrow in part payment for one-third interest in the town site of Decrows Point.

In April, we moved into our new frame house of eight rooms and three stories. The house was very substantially built, and was calculated to resist a very considerable storm. It was very roomy and commanded a fine view of both the bay and the gulf. We had been living for three months previously in the kichen and outhouses of this building. So we all enjoyed greatly the new, clean, cool, roomy house. We lived well on the coast, had any quantity of fish, always fine, had fruits fresh from New Orleans and splendid gardens and the best water melons in the world and never suffered from the heat· And still we were aware great storms might come and destructive cyclones at equinoxial times, and we often talked of going back to San Antonio.

April 13th, we heard General Scott was marching from Vera Cruz towards the City of Mexico.

April 12th, Mr. Maverick went to Matagorda to try the galvanic battery on his still suffering shoulder, and returned the 16th, much benefitted.

April 22nd, Mr. Maverick left for San Antonio to be gone three weeks. He wrote me that Colonel Hays was married on April 24th, at Seguin to Miss Susan Calvert, and that on May 1st, a large party of San Antonians met them on the Salado and gave them a grand ovation. Mr. Giulbeau gave a party and reception to Colonel Hays and bride. Mr. Maverick mentioned that six or seven hundred soldiers were mustering at San Antonio, to be formed into a regiment and to march to Mexico under Colonel Hays, and stated also that there was a great increase in the American population of the town.

April 25th, we all took a trip to Tiltona, Cora Vandever and Mr. Peck accompanying us. The girls were on horseback, and I with the children in the cart with Mr. Peck driving. We spent a delightful week drinking fresh milk, fishing, bathing in the breakers, riding and having a general good time. We returned May 1st, and took home with us chickens and turkeys, butter and eggs, fresh beef and other farm products.

May 1st, fourteen lots were sold for eight hundred dollars in "Cahoun" across the Pass.

May 2nd, $1200.00 worth of lots were sold here in Paso Cavallo, and it seems they are to be improved.

July 3d, Mrs. Vandever and I with the girls and escorted by Major Stores and Captain Cummings, went to Lavaca to attend the Grand Fourth of July Ball. Mr. Maverick remained at home with the children. At Lavaca the girls had numerous beaux and a fine time. We returned by the way of Dutch town (now Indianola) a thriving place, and at that time threatening to deprive Lavaca of her large trade. At Lavaca we stopped at Mrs. Eberle's and at Dutch Town with the family of Reverend Mr. Blair. July 15th, we took a boat and visited our farm Tiltona, returning on the 26th.   Robert J. Clow and John Mann courted Lizzie, who had much attention—they both got "no" for their answer, but Bob Clow said he believed she meant "yes" for him. September, Cora Vandever was married to Billy Nichols, a pilot and a good man.

Chapter XIV.

THE ANGEL OF DEATH.

BUT after all the Peninsula was not home to us in the full sense of that word. Mr. Maverick was constantly returning to San Antonio on business, and on each visit he was making new investments and knitting his interest and his sentiments more and more with the life and growth of San Antonio and the surrounding country. To me the four years of our early married life spent in San Antonio seemed like a bright vision—a veritable romance. The memory of the stirring events of that period and of the birth of my Lewis and Agatha there, kept my affections warm for the dear old place.

On the 15th day of October 1847, with bag and baggage, we left the Point and set off for San Antonio. It was right sad to leave a pleasant home and the friends we had gathered during three years, and not the least regret was it to say goodbye to Mr. Peck, who had taught our children faithfully for two years and been a member of our household, but his health was re-established and he obeyed the urgent requests of his mother to return to her in his native state. He was quite anxious to go with us to San Antonio, but he parted with us at the Pass and returned to Ohio.

At Lavaca we stopped at Mrs. Staunton's until the 19th, when Lizzie and I, with Agatha, and George and his nurse Betsy took the stage for San Antonio—my first stage ride in Texas. Mr. Maverick, Sam, Lewis and the servants took passage with the wagons and our household goods and we did not see them again until November 4th. We spent the first night in Victoria with Maggie Pearson, the

second in Cuero at Cardwell's. On the 21st, we stopped in
Gonzales with Mrs. Brown. It rained all night and until
nine the next morning. The 22nd, we went only a short
distance and stopped with old lady Trimble. Mrs. Trimble had lived here over twenty years, and had herself
fought the Indians. Her first husband had been killed,
and her second husband fell in the Alamo. Three months
after his death, she gave birth to twin girls, now eleven
years old. An older daughter's husband had fallen with
Dawson and she had given birth, seven weeks after his
death to a girl and had died. The pretty child was five
years old when we were there and the idol of her fond
grandmother.

The 23rd, we reached New Braunfels at the junction
of the Comal with the Guadalupe. This was a pretty
place, and rapidly filling up, and I thought the Comal the
lovliest stream I ever saw.

Sunday, October 24th, at three p. m., we arrived in San
Antonio, and stopped at Aunt Ann Bradley's at the south
east corner of Commerce and Yturri Streets—everything
covered with dust and the heat dreadful. The town seemed much changed since 1842; many strangers had settled
here and immigrants were arriving daily. Not until
November 4th, did Mr. Maverick's party arrive—the hired
wagoners insisted on stopping five days at their home on
the way, and I had time to grow very uneasy about them
—but all were well and we moved directly into our old
home with its dirt floors, for the cement had all worn off.
The fence around the garden was nearly gone and the
garden itself was in a dilapidated condition, but the figs
and the pomegranates were still standing. The weather
grew quite cold, and we learned that many people were
sick with colds and diarrhea, and almost every day some-
body died, which made us quite doleful. I recalled our
first residence in San Antonio, and it seemed that in those
days there was scarcely any sickness and postively no
case of fever, save the case of Colonel Karnes which was

yellow fever imported from Houston. Now, all of our children suffered some illness.

Late in November, Lewis was spinning a top at the front door and George was sitting on the door sill, when Lewis' top bounced up and struck George on the forehead. George went into spasms, but we packed him in a wet sheet and blankets and he got well, but he was quite low for a week or so and he has ever retained the scar.

December first, brother Andrew, surgeon in Captain Veach's company, spent a few days with us on his way to the Rio Grande.

On Friday, December 24th, our sixth child, Willie H., was born. The joyous bells of Christmas Eve were ringing when he was born.

1848.

April 4th, 1848, Mr. Maverick left with Mr. Tivy, deputy surveyor, and a considerable surveying party, to have a pet location on Las Moras creek surveyed. He located our headright certificate on the head spring, and Fort Clark is on that tract—he also located much land below that survey.

April 29th, Mr. Clow came to marry Lizzie, although she has not set the day.

The Angel of Death. Sunday, April 30th, my dear little Agatha took fever. Lizzie and I with the girls and Betsy with the baby were out walking and we were near the Mill Bridge when she first complained. I told Betsy to take baby and go home with her, when Agatha said: "O, if my papa was here he would carry me." At this time Agatha was a large and very beautiful child of seven years. She was the idol of her father, and in return for his devoted affection for her, she idolized him. The sentiment of love between Mr. Maverick and the sweet child was something extraordinary, something beautiful and touching to behold.

When I got home, I bathed her in tepid water and cared tenderly for her, but on the following day she grew much

SAN ANTONIO RIVER BACK OF TWOHIG HOME

worse, and I called in the services of Dr. Cupples. He gave her an emetic and then powders and enemas, but nothing seemed to reduce the fever or overcome the stupor. Day by day, Dr. Cupples encouraged me to hope, but I lost my appetite and passed many sleepless nights, for a terrible fear took possession of me. My fears whispered in my heart, "Agatha is dying," and I lost hope.

The poor child, with crimson cheek and shining eyes, sometimes raved wildly—once she screamed out in agonizing manner: "Oh, Sam," she thought she saw Indians about to kill Sam. When she took her medicine, (the first in her life)· she would say: "Mamma, will you tell papa I was good and took my medicine?" Once she said, "Mamma if I die————" but I could not bear it—I stopped her before she could speak another word. Ah, how often have I regretted my action, and fondly longed to know what the dear angel would have told me. Her father was still out on his surveying expedition on the Las Moras, and we had no means of cummunicating with him. On May 8th, the poor child breathed her last at two a. m., Tuesday, May 9th, 1848. Even now, in 1880, after thirty-two years, I cannot dwell on that terrible bereavement. The child was the perfection of sweetness and beauty and possessed such a glad and joyous disposition that her very presence was a flood of sunshine.

On May 12th, Augusta took the same bilious fever, which quite a number of people in the town had at the time. Dr. Sturgis came and treated her for two days, when she recovered and in a short while became quite well again. We now learned from the servants that our nurse Lavinia and Mrs. Bradley's nurse had taken Agatha and Augusta and Mrs. Bradley's girls Pauline and Ada, on April 25th, out walking and had allowed them to eat as many green mustang grapes as they would. I have always attributed Agatha's death and Augusta's deadly sickness to the grapes. Pauline and Ada had similar attacks about the same time but not as severe as Augusta's.

Tuesday, May 23rd, at 7:30 a. m. Lizzie was married to

Mr. Clow, Reverend Mr. McCulloch officiating, and at eight a. m. took the stage for Saluria.

Friday, May 26th, Mr. Maverick returned. Eleven miles west of town, he met an acquaintance who told him of Agatha's death! He went to the grave and threw himself down upon it ,and remained there until it was dark. No one but God could tell the depth of his anguish. He was crushed and broken when he came home. He said he was striving "not to murmur at the will of God." He said we should humble ourselves in sack cloth and ashes —and he never removed that sack cloth in spirit whilst he lived—was ever after a sad changed man.

That night I dreamed so distinctly that Agatha ran through our room and out at the door again—the dream seemed so real that I jumped up, and looked for her with a candle in my hand, in spite of reason. And Mr. Maverick said: "She has wandered off in the dark and we will never on earth be able to find her." Another time in his deep anguish he said: "Cursed land, cursed money, I would give all, all, only to see her once more."

May 29th, Mr. Maverick wrote a touching letter to his father telling him of our loss—one of his sentences was this: "I feel as if, every moment, she is being torn out of my heart."

My poor little Willie came near starving to death when Agatha was sick and after her death—my milk almost dried up. I got Mrs. Elliott's cook, Patience, to nurse him two weeks, and then had to begin feeding him. This disagreed with him, and all summer he was very sick and thin and fretful—once he lay at the point of death with the dysentery, and the doctor told Mrs. Elliott there was no hope. Mrs. Gorch told me to make tea of pomegranate root, and give a teaspoonful every fifteen minutes until the dysentery was checked. I did this and I believe it saved his life. As he grew better and well, it was wonderful how he liked his hoarhound tea and drank goats milk.

August 13th, read in the Pendleton Messenger of July 7th, the following obituary:

Departed this life, Agatha Maverick, at San Antonio, Texas, on the 9th of May, aged seven years and twenty-seven days, eldest daughter of Samuel A. and Mary A. Maverick. "Oh, Almighty and all just God, teach us how it is that the poor little boon of the breath of life, could not be spared from thy great storehouse to animate a little dear thing which thou hast made so perfect."

The portion in quotation marks is an extract from Mr. Maverick's letter.

Poor little Augusta missed her sister "Tita" so much, and, as we grieved without ceasing, so did she. Daily she gathered flowers and kept them in water until the afternoon, and then she took them to the grave for "Tita"— Tita who had ever been her companion and her ideal of goodness.

Augusta was a child of great promise, gentle, patient, thoughtful, and pious beyond her years. She was very fair with blue eyes and light hair, and she had a high, broad forehead and a development of mind beyond her age. She was very fond of attending Sunday School, and of listening to singing and of caring for the baby—and was always obedient. She repeated her prayers nightly and was ever talking of God and his angels and of "our Tita with them."

Ah, pure and spotless angel, thyself.

In August Colonel Hays was ordered to open a shorter and better trading route through the wilds to Chihuahua, Mexico. Colonel Hays asked me to persaude Mr. Maverick to go with the expedition. I answered: "Oh, no, he is not well enough for such a hard trip." Then Hays replied, "Don't you see Mr. Maverick is dying by inches? Every one remarks how gray he has grown, how bent and feeble he looks, and this will be the very thing for him— he always thrives on hardships, and his mind must be distracted now from his grief."

I recognized the truth and force of this reasoning and

that Hays loved him dearly and I set to work to persuade him to go. My husband was quite reasonable, and quickly saw that the trip had become a necessity for him.

On Sunday, August 27th, Mr. Maverick left with Colonel Hays, fifty men and fifteen Delaware Indian guides, to run out the new route to Chihuahua. They had a very severe trip, especially going—they got lost and were nearly starved and their horses suffered more severely than the men. One man lost his reason and was lost and afterwards saved by the Indians and recovered. While hopelessly lost ,they met some Indians from Santa Fe who sold them some bread and peloncillos and pointed out to them the road to San Carlos on the Rio Grande; where they arrived a few days after.

Their return trip was much shorter. A good road, comparatively, was surveyed of about seven hundred miles from El Paso to San Antonio.

They were greatly troubled on their return by the Indians hanging about, and trying to stampede their horses and they had one fight with them.

They got back Sunday, December 10th, and the three and a half months of hardship had done wonders for Mr. Maverick, just as Colonel Hays had thought. He said that Mr. Maverick had been the "most enduring and least complaining man of the party," had encouraged others, walked much to save his horse—had cheerfully eaten roots, berries, mule-meat and polecats, and had chewed leather and the tops of his boots, to keep his mouth moist when no water could be found. Besides coming back in good health Mr. Maverick was more cheerful and hopeful.

A ball was given to Hays and his company, and another to the officers of the United States Army stationed here, but we did not go.

Christmas was beautiful—glad day of redemption to the world.

1849.

Cholera. New Years Day was bright and beautiful,

but we heard the cholera had appeared in New Orleans. We also heard at the same time that some bad mess pork had caused the death of a hundred soldiers recently landed at Lavaca, and destined for this place—frightful! Some think it cholera.

And here in San Antonio violent influenza with sore throat and measles and scarletina were prevailing. Pallas, Aunt Ann's house boy, died—he told his mother: "God came to me in a dream, and took me to heaven," and he asked her to pray with him and then he died.

February 28th, Major Chevalier took small pox at Aunt Ann's, and was sent to an isolated room in the yard and nursed there. Russell Howard, one of the volunteer nurses, took the disease from him.

March 7th, sister Lizzie came, spent five days with me and went back to Mr. Clow in Lavaca. March 29th, Mrs. Elliott, Mrs. Lockwood and I sat up all night with Mrs. Richardson, mother of Mrs. Judge Paschal, and closed her eyes in death. Heard of the death of George Peacock and four others of cholera in Lavaca. We talked of going into the country and camping out, before the cholera reached San Antonio—this we made up our minds to do, but the weather was very bad, wind and rain and fog, continually, and we waited for better weather—alas! too long.

Monday the second of April, cholera appeared in San Antonio. For two weeks it was confined to Mexicans in low, damp places, and Dr. Cupples thought it was easily managed and would not become epidemic, but suddenly, in gloom overhead and in our hearts it appeared everywhere in the most violent form and would not yield to treatment. April 22nd, twenty-one died of cholera.

Death of Augusta. On Monday 23rd, O, world of grief! my darling Augusta complained of colic in the evening—it was damp and cold. We gave her the remedies which were ready in every house and she felt pretty well and went to sleep a perfect picture of rosy health and beauty. About midnight she awoke vomiting and purging violently. Dr. Sturgis was down with the cholera and we called in two other physicians, but all that could be done gave no relief.

God willed to take our darling. In four hours, her case was pronounced hopeless and she looked thin and emaciated, purple and sunken, but conscious to the last, and suffering fearfully. We humbly gave her up, beseeching God to stay the hand of the pestilence, for Lewis and George were both attacked at daylight. At eight a. m., Augusta felt no more pain and tried to get out of bed; at nine o'clock, one hour afterwards, she breathed her last. She was six years and twenty-five days old. They buried her the next day by the side of Tita—I could not go.

Two nights before her attack, Augusta had a lovely dream, which made me tremble when she related it to me on Saturday morning, she smiling and happy the while over its loveliness. In her dream she was clothed in a new dress, all white and shining and flowing down below her feet. She got into a carriage and with a large procession went "way off to a big church" resounding with sweet music, and filled with people dressed in white. It was prophesy of her shroud and burial and resurrection.

God I thank Thee that we could yield her up unsullied by earth—her memory a white and shining light.

Just before she died, knowing she had only a few moments to live, I took her in my arms and held her in my lap before the fire, and said to her: "Gussie, do you know our Father in Heaven?" "Oh, yes, mamma," she answered earnestly. She said: "I hear then singing, mamma, put my bonnet on and let me go to church." I put the little fresh muslin bonnet on her head. She loved the bonnet and was content—she looked up, listened intently, and said: "Don't you hear them, mamma?"

"Gussie, do you want to see God?"

"Yes, Mamma."

"Do you want to see Tita?"

"Yes, mama." And these were her last words.
Thou wert purity itself my gentle child.

Death had no terrors for thee,

The gates of Heaven were open for thee:

Whilst yet in the flesh, thou didst behold thy Father's
face in Heaven.

On the day of Augusta's death, Lewis and George both
had the cholera. The doctors were prompt and their
cases yielded to treatment, although George was very
low for awhile. I also was threatened and had to go to
bed by George's side and take my medicine like the
others. On that day, many children died, two of whom
were friends and playmates of Augusta. Of our servants,
Granville, Emmeline and Ann had the cholera, and in fact
every soul of the household except Sam and Betsy was
more or less affected. Idle would be the task of portray-
ing the gloom of our household, or the terror which seized
upon the community. Fear and dread were in every house
—an oppressive weight in the atmosphere. Into every
house came the pestilence, in most houses was death, and
in some families one-half died! All had symptoms and
the weather continued close and damp and dismal. Men
of strong nerve and undoubted courage shrank in fear—
many drank hard and died drunk—some dropped and
died in the streets—one poor fellow cut his throat when
attacked. Never can those who were here in that terrible
visitation forget its gloom and horror. The cholera lasted six weeks ,and the priests thought that over six hundred people died. One third of the population fled to
the ranchos and into the country and they generally got
above this heavy atmosphere and escaped.

July 10th, Mr. Maverick sent me with the four boys and
Betsy to Sutherland Springs to rest and recuperate. We
stopped first at Dr. Sutherlands, and Mrs. Frank Pashal
with her three children stopped at Mrs. Johnson's. Mrs.
Sutherland was very kind to us, but as all the water
there was mineral, we moved to Mrs. Johnson's and drank
Chalybeate water. Mrs. Johnson's little daughter died

of convulsions while we were there.   We felt no improvement by our visit to the springs.   A number of strangers were there from the low country, some housed and some camping, and there was much sickness—all the log cabins were full of the sick.   On the 17th, Mrs. Paschal took the stage for San Antonio, and on the 19th, I did the same.

COMMERCE STREET IN THE 60'S, LOOKING EAST

Chapter XV.

OUR NEW HOME ON ALAMO PLAZA.

I felt that I could not live any longer at the old place, and Mr. Maverick, too, did not want to live there. We concluded that the high ground on the Alamo Plaza would be a more healthful location. When Mr. Maverick sent us to the springs, he remained in San Antonio to move our household goods from the old home to an old Mexican house he had bought on the Alamo Plaza, and also to make arrangements for building us a new two-story house.

When we returned to San Antonio, on July 19th, 1849, we settled down in the old house I have mentioned, and did the best we could. This house was situated on the lot now formed by the west line of Alamo Plaza and the south line of Houston Street. At that time, and for some years thereafter Houston (Paseo) Street was not in existence.

Heavenly Comfort. On September 1st, I had a sweet, consoling dream. Agatha and Augusta came from the Spirit-Land to comfort me. I took Augusta in my arms, and clothed her in white robes. Then I asked to see Agatha, and she stood in the window, a little taller than in life—I clasped her in my arms. They told me they were very happy, and said we should be together in Heaven.

Singular how real it was, and how happy and thankful it made me.

September 30th, I heard an excellent sermon by Mr. Fish, the Army Chaplain, on the parent's duty of training their children in the way they should go—with the blessed promise, "and when they are old they will not depart from it." October 21st, Reverend Ambrose Smith preached his farewell sermon—I Thes. XI., 11. November 4th, Reverend Mr. Fish preached a splendid sermon—II Cor. IV, 7.

September 5th, Mr. Maverick's nephew, Augustus W. Wayman, died of cholera at West Point—his four years' cadetship nearly completed.

November 5th, Mrs. Elliott, Susan Hays and I had our daguerrotypes taken at Whitfield's gallery—Mrs. Hays is going to California to join her husband. Susan and I had joined the Methodist Episcopal Church in '48, during our husband's absence on the expedition to open a better route to Chihuahua. She preferred that church, but I only joined till my own, theProtestant Episcopal, should be established here, and we had been great friends, and "sisters" ever since, though she was so much younger. On Christmas Day, Mr. Young, the local Methodist minister for two years past, dined with us and said goodbye. He was going home to Mississippi—an earnest and zealous Christian and much beloved here.

1850.

Wednesday, February 6th, at ten p. m., was born our seventh child, John Hays. John was an old name in the Maverick family—Hays was in honor of our friend the Colonel. The baby and Willie were baptized on April 4th, by Bishop G. W. Freeman, of Louisiana. Sam, Lewis, Agatha, Augusta and George had been baptized at Decrows Point by the Reverend Caleb Ives of Matagorda. Johnnie looked so delicate that scarcely any one thought he could live. But I hoped on, and devoted my time day and night to him, and he was seldom out of my arms.

July 19th, he had a sudden attack of cholera infantum, and died before night—"Thy will be done." . . .

In July, Mr. Schmidt commenced building our new house of stone and built very fast.

September 10th, Bombre began the carpenter work.

September 15th. Susan Hays spent a day and night

with me. She was as lovely and lovable as ever. She was to start in two weeks to join her hero-husband in California.

25th, Mary Bradley returned with Major Tom Howard and wife and baby Fannie.

29th, we and all old San Antonios bid Mrs. Hays goodbye—Bob Hays and Mr. Randall go with her.

Saturday October 5th. Lewis was gathering pecans, when a rotten limb broke with his weight and he fell to the ground breaking both bones in his right arm, just above the wrist. Although it was a mile below town, he walked home—accompanied by Joe, Mrs. Elliott's black boy. Dr.Dignowity set his arm. Lewis suffered much pain and I sat by him all night pouring cold water over his arm. The next day, Sunday, Dr. Dignowity put his arm in a tin sheath and he slept little—Monday night no sleep—Tuesday night the same. Wednesday he was better, slept some and enjoyed seeing the children at their play. Thursday he walked some with his arm in a sling. Friday the pain returned and sleeplessness—feverish and groaning—again I poured cold water all night. Monday 14th; the bandages and tin sheath were taken off, and we found an abcess below the elbow. I was frightened; it looked like gangrene. But the doctor said it was all right, applied a poultice with "number six" and gave a "course." The swelling subsided and he slowly got over his suffering—but not before the 30th of November did he have any use of his arm—and it is not straight.

December 1st, 1850. We moved into our new house and found it very nice, after the old Mexican quarters we had occupied over a year. The new house, considerably enlarged, is standing today, and is now known as the Maverick Homestead.*

1851.

Mr. Maverick took Lewis to the Army Surgeon, Dr. Wright, to have his arm straightened, but it was too late.

*Where Gibbs Building now stands, Avenue D and Houston Streets.

March 16th. I am thirty-three years old today, and am trying to keep Lent. Sunday April 13th, after evening service, I was confirmed by Bishop Freeman of Louisiana.

A New Daughter. On Tuesday, June 17th, 1851, at eight a. m. was born our third daughter, Màry Brown. How glad and thankful were Mr. Maverick and I to have a daughter. She was named for Father Maverick's "blessed grandmother "Mary Brown."*

Soon after Mary's birth, I wasted until I fainted twice and grew quite helpless and almost speechless. This was caused by the mid-wife Mrs. D., wilfully giving me lobelia —telling me it was raspberry tea. I felt my hold on life very slight, but in my fainting had felt an indescribable peace. For two weeks I could scarcely move without fainting, but after that I grew strong very fast. My precious baby grew thin the while, and Mrs. Beck, who had a baby born on the same day with mine, nursed Mary twice a day. Mary was sent to her each morning and afternoon for five or six weeks. When Mary was seven weeks old, we had to commence feeding her, and I began drinking ale and porter myself to see whether I could provide the proper nourishment—and I recovered my strength rapidly. Baby however, was thin and fretful.

Mr. Maverick had been elected to the Legislature, and he wished to visit his father who had been stricken with paralysis, but he did not see how he could leave us.

August 23rd. We call in the services of a goat—feed it well—and milk it four or five times a day for baby, and she improves some.

Bone Soup Bath. August 28th, Mrs. Salsmon, an experienced German nurse, came to see baby, and persuaded me to bathe her daily in bone soup. The bone soup

*Samuel Maverick (1772-1852) always spoke of this grandmother, Mary Turpin Brown of Providence, R. I., as his "blessed grandmother Mary Brown" and at mention of her name bared his head; this gratitude was well deserved for during Revolutionary days when his father was a prisoner on the Jersey Prison ship and their home destroyed by the British, his mother took the family to this same grandmother who cared for them tenderly until it was possible for their return to Charleston. She was a Quaker, as were her people.

is made by boiling beef bones four hours, and then cooling to a temperature of about one hundred, and the bath is ready. Daily I put her into the bath, and kept her there some time, and then, while wet from the bath, rolled her in a blanket and put her to sleep. And when she awaked, I rubbed her well and dressed her. At first the bath did not seem to do any good. But Mr. Maverick asked me to try it one month, and then we saw she had steadily improved. The treatment was kept up for about six months.

Mr. Maverick bought a horse and buggy and drove us out into the country every evening.

September 28th, baby is rosy and playful and good. November 2nd, Mr. Maverick weighed baby before leaving on the morrow for Austin—she weighed ten and half pounds, and we were happy over it. She was growing good sized like any other baby, and I began to feed her rice and hominy water in her milk—also soup. Mr. Maverick writes often and is always solicitous about his daughter.

The Houstons Come.   November 31st, Dr. Houston and Routez Houston, his wife, with their three children, Hannah Jane, Mary Elizabeth and Augustus W., and with wagons and negroes, arrive from North Alabama to settle in Texas—and they stay with us until after the holidays. Ross Houston with his household camped on the Cibolo.

December 30th, Mr. Maverick came over from Austin to spend Christmas with us, and we all enjoyed the holidays and the children Santa Claus' visit.

1852.

January 3d, 1852, Dr. Houston took his family to the new house on the Cibolo about twenty-seven miles E. S. E. from San Antonio. Ross Houston built his house one mile nearer San Antonio.

January 5th, Maley caught cold and became quite sick and was not well again until the 26th, when she recovered her health and became playful and fat, and weighed

thirteen and a half pounds. How miserable and frightened I was when she was ill. During January, we stopped
using the bone soup bath.

February 15th. Baby and I were out riding and Lewis
was driving the mare, when some one discharged a gun
near us which frightened the mare and she ran away
kicking and charging wildly. We, Lewis and I, together,
turned her head against a fence, when she reared and fell
back on the buggy and broke a shaft. I jumped out with
baby and the men who had been shooting ran to our assistance. Mr. Teagle helped us to repair the shaft and
drove us home.

February 16th, Maley cut her first tooth and was not
sick. 17th, weighed fourteen and a half pounds. 20th,
had another tooth. 22nd, Mr. Maverick got home. March
17th, Maley weighed fifteen pounds. April 17th, sixteen pounds. May 17th, seventeen pounds.

On April 20th, Maley not very well. 22nd, Mary Brown
was baptized by Bishop G. W. Freeman. May 1st, we all
attended a picnic at San Pedro Springs. Willie narrow-
ly escaped being run over by Judge Paschal's coach.

Father Maverick's Death. May 7th, received a letter
from Mr. Maverick's sister, Lydia A. Van Wyck, saying
father was better and could whisper. 15th, another letter said he was very sick. 22nd, Mr. Maverick received a
letter from a cousin, Robert Maxwell, giving the sad tid-
ings of father Maverick's death—he died April 28th,
1852. The poor old man suffered over two years before
he died. His son never ceased to regret that he did not go
on to see him, ere he died—but he seemed to be tied here
all the while, still hoping to start soon, and yet finding
something to detain him.

June 17th, Mary, one year old, weighs seventeen and
a half pounds. Mrs. Samuel made her a pretty dotted
swiss dress. Mary can stand alone—is happy and playful. Sam and Lewis went down to Cibolo to visit the
Houstons.

July 5th, Routez came up to see us.

July 13th, my sister with her two girls, Kate and Alice, and nurse, came up from the coast to pay us a good long visit.

October 6th, Mr. Clow came up, spent a week with us and took his family home. Lizzie sent me an old china bowl, an heirloom in our family, which has descended through five generations that we know of, each time to the youngest daughter . Mrs. Agatha Strother owned it, and it is said in our family tradition she inherited it. From Agatha Strother it descended to Mrs. A. Madison—from her to Mrs. Lucy Lewis—from her to Mrs. Agatha L. Adams—from her to Mrs. Elizabeth Clow—from her to Ada Clow, her youngest daughter. (Lizzie wanted me to keep it in my family, but in 1879 I sent it to Ada Clow by my son Willie H. Maverick.)

1853.

January 4th, 1853, Mr. Maverick being away at the Legislature in Austin, I took all the children and left on the stage at ten p. m. for Dr. Houston's. There we had a delightful visit. Heard of Fleming Bradley's death, and his mother's great grief and distress. February 8th, we returned from the Cibolo, and found the heavy snow of the 6th, still unmelted. The excessive cold and the snow together had cracked our cement roof and it was leaking badly. February 13th, thermometer down to twelve degrees above zero at three a. m. Mr. Maverick got home on the stage quite ill with bilious colic. Althoug he had been quite ill at Austin for two weeks, he continued, without complaining, to attend to his legislative duties. He now submitted to a "botanic course" and kept in bed for several days—wonderful for him.

March 9th, Mr. Maverick went with John McDonald surveying to Fort Mason and the Llano, and to Fort Chadbourne and the Red Fork of the Colorado.

March 18th. X. B. Saunders held an examination at his school and our boys received prizes. We gave Mr.

Saunders his board to help him and he to help our boys—
fair exchange. Judge Saunders is now residing at Bel-
ton, Texas. George tells me that Mr. Saunders used to
spank him daily, never omitting a school day, but that he
did not "lay it on hard."

April 25th, Mr. Maverick returned in good health.

May 1st, Sam and Lewis attend dancing school.

May 17th, Colonel Dancy took dinner with us, and in
the evening we all had a gay time trying "table rapping."
Colonel Dancy was a spiritual medium—and he told me
I was a medium also.

May 18th, George had the mumps. June 5th, Mary
had mumps but she was not sick, and she laughed at
"mamma's baby" in the glass.

June 21st, Willie makes his first trip to school—with
George.

June 28th, sat up all night with Mrs. Cox who is dying.
She is mother of Mrs. Ogden.

In July, a committee of six ladies were chosen to get up
a church supper, in order to raise funds to complete the
Methodist Church on Soledad Street.

On July 28th, our supper came off—we worked very
hard, and the supper was renewed the second night. The
sum of $617.00 was netted, and turned over to the build-
ing committee of which Elder Whipple was president,
and Miss Harriett Richardson treasurer.

August 21, we heard that yellow fever was very bad in
New Orleans.

November 4th, Mr. Maverick attended the Legislature
at Austin. Sam and Lewis came back from a long visit
to the Cibolo—they had beaten all hands picking cotton. General Rusk, United States Senator from Texas,
visited San Antonio, in November. He dined with me—
we went to the Theatre at the Casino, then on south side
of Dolorosa Street, near the present location of Hord's
Hotel, and saw the laughter-provoking play of "Bombas-
tes Furioso."

December 22nd. An Episcopal supper was given in

the old Alamo Chuch—the weather was bad, and the venture brought us no return.

1854.

January 1854.   Sam, Lewis and I joined Professor Ryan's class in Psychology.   March 15th, Mary Elliott married Russell Howard.   I received a letter from brother Andrew, written at Huepac, Sonora, Mexico.

Conquista Ranch Established.   On March 29th, Mr. Maverick with Sam and Lewis, and Granville and four Mexicans set off for our old Tiltona Rancho on the Matagorda Peninsula, with the purpose of bringing Jinny and her children and the stock cattle to a tract of land on the left bank of the San Antonio River, about forty-five miles below San Antonio.   The new location afterwards called by us the Conquista Ranch, because the noted Conquista ford of the river was on this tract.   The tract extended along the river from a point half a mile above the Conquista ford to a point below the mouth of Marcellino Creek.   They were gone two months, had a rough, hard time of it and all came back well and hearty on May 24th.

On Sunday, May 7th, 1854, was born our ninth child, Albert.   I was very weak and did not have milk enough for him.   In August Mr. Maverick established Conquista Ranch in due form—built a house, fences and pens and left Jack in charge of the place.   On August 14th, Sam and Lewis with Mr. Maverick went down to the ranch. Joey Thompson and Lizzie Houston spent December with us and we enjoyed the time very much.

1855.

March 1855, Joey Thompson and Lizzie Houston came to pay us a long visit.   In April, I gave them a party which the girls enjoyed very much.   We had a large company and the girls received great attention.   In the latter part of August, our whole family went down to visit the Houstons and to partake of a birthday dinner given to Joey Thompson.   While at the Houstons, we had a great Indian scare. A party of some twenty-five or thirty Comanches made a raid down the Cibolo, crossed the San Antonio River at the Conquista ford, and by rapid marches escaped to the mountains with impunity. They killed two persons, stole some horses and killed others. My boys, Sam and Lewis, joined the party which went in pursuit of the Indians, and I became wretched and anxious about them.

Sebastopol. Wild rumors came soon after the boys had gone, to the effect that several hundred warriors had been seen not many mles from Dr. Hodston's house. This was a new and startling turn. Dr. Houston's house was a large and substantial stone building and the people for miles around crowded there. We fortified the house and most of us kept awake the whole night. We dubbed the place, in its fortified condition, "Sebastopol," which indicated our intention to defend ourselves to the last. But it all proved a mere scare of some easily frightened person.

While on this visit to the Houstons, we went up to a grand ball at Seguin, and to dinner and speeches the next day.

In December, Mr. Maverick was attending the Senate in Austin, when we concluded to pay him a visit. On December 20th, I with George, Willie, Mary and Albert and nurse Betsy, accompanied by Joey Houston, went over to Austin to visit Mr. Maverick, and attend the inaugural of Governor Pease. We boarded at Mrs. Newell's and had a nice visit of two or three weeks. Joey made a decided "impression." She played and sang well, and was very attractive and lively and she had several offers of marriage to consider and decline before we left Austin.

1856.

We returned from Austin about January 10th, 1856, and on the 12th, we went with Joey to Dr. Houston's. Sam Thompson, her brother, fifteen years old then, was there. He, on February 20th, 1856, took her back home to North Alabama. Colonel and Susan Hays and their two interesting children, Jack and Dickey, visited San Antonio and the Calverts at Seguin.

February 14th, Mr. Maverick returned from Austin. While in Austin, to please Jack, he bought Rosetta, Jack's wife, and her three children and brought them along with him in the stage.

April 19th, Mr. Maverick went with J. McDonald and eleven others surveying on the San Saba and up on the Red Fork of the Colorado, to be gone two months. Mr. Maverick returned June 11th. William McDonald accidentally shot himself in camp.

Separation. On June 22nd, 1856, Lewis, then seventeen years of age, left us to go to college in Burlington, Vermont. I felt as if some dear one had died, and I missed my dear Lewis dreadfhlly.

July 3d, George was bit on the left foot by a moccasin snake, whilst bathing above town at the island, now the Grand Avenue crossing. Sam cut the wound and sucked the poison from it. George ran home and we had a great fright. Dr. Herff* gave him whisky, and he got over it in a few weeks.

In September, Mr. Maverick sold to Mr. A. Toutant Beaureguard all his cattle, estimated at four hundred head. They were at Conquista ranch and scattered over the country around there.

September 24th, 1856, Mr. Maverick set off with Sam; Mr. Maverick on business for the S. A. & M. A. Railway Company, and Sam for college. It was hard to let Sam go —he and Lewis so far away. On the day they left, Willie ran a nail into his heel and I was alarmed, but Willie got through safely. Mr. Maverick and Sam visited Lewis in Vermont, and Lewis ran down with them to New York City.

On November 8th, Sam sailed for Europe to attend the University of Edinboro in Scotland—across the ocean!

---

*Dr. Ferdinand Herff, skilled physician, came to San Antonio from Germany in 1847, member of an independent political society consisting of young Germans of the upper class.

1857—1859.

Birth and Death of Our Tenth Child.   On October 17th, 1857, our fourth daughter and tenth and last child, Elizabeth, was born, a very delicate baby.

We did everything we could to save her life, but all in vain.   She died March 28th, 1859, aged one year, five months, and eleven days.

Chapter XVI.

CONCLUSION.

THE task I set out to perform is completed. With the death of my last child, I closed the book of the past—the remoter past—and the events which have happened since 1859, seem too modern to be incorporated into this book. But in order to connect the remoter past with the actual present I feel that I ought to take a rapid glance over the period of twenty-two years which has intervened.

The Civil War soon came on and Mr. Maverick and my sons did not shrink from what they conceived to be their duty. Mr. Maverick had always been a Union man in sentiment, he loved the Union of the states, and although he may have believed (before the question was settled) that we had the abstract right to withdraw from the Union, he thought the Union was sacred, and that the idea of a dissolution of the Union ought not to be harbored for a moment. Having such ideas and convictions, he found life to be uncongenial and unpromising for him in South Carolina, where the doctrines of nullification and ultimate secession were agressively espoused by an overwhelming majority of the ruling class. He came to Texas, but all doctrines and issues of the former time bloomed into life about him when Texas became a member of the union. Creeping beneath the shadow of the manifold blessings of the Union, came the bitter and unceasing strife. At last he came to believe the quarrel was forced upon us, and that there was before us an "irressible ronflict" which we could not escape, no matter where we turned·

The Secession Convention of 1861 met—there was intense excitement and, need I say, deep gloom—the hour

came at last when he was compelled to take his choice for
or against his kith and kin.   The question was no longer
whether secession was right or wrong, wise or unwise,
the question was now narrowed down to this—Even if
you could sever your fate from that of your people,
would your heart permit you to do it?

Thus it appeared to him, and he did a simple, straight-
forward unselfish act, and an act which nevertheless
gave him deep pain, when he cast his vote for secession.

The boys—well, their youthful and warm sympathies
were aroused, and a simple sense of duty carried them
hand and heart with their state. When the war commenced, Lewis was attending Chapel Hill, University of North
Carolina—he immediately enlisted for six months in the
1st North Alabama Regiment, and was at Big Bethel,
the first battle of the war.   Sam had returned from college—he enlisted in the 1st Texas Cavalry, under Colonel
Henry McCulloch, which regiment served on the Indian
frontier for one year.   In 1862, Sam crossed the Mississippi River and attached himself to the 8th Texas Cavalry,
the gallant Terry Rangers.   With that regiment he served
until the war was ended and, whilst with them, he gained
many laurels, for tireless devotion and unflinching courage.   Lewis returned to us at the end of his first en-
listment, and raised a company, Company "E", for the
32nd Texas Cavalry commanded by Colonel Woods. When
the company was mustered in, April, 1862, George at the
age of sixteen was sworn in with the rest as a private in
his brother's company.   George remained a soldier and
a private throughout the war.   Lewis was promoted during 1864, to the staff of General DeBray, with the rank
of Major. At the battle of Blair's Landing on Red River,
on the — day of April, 1864, Lewis received a severe
wound in the leg and George a slight scratch on his left
ear. Sam was "scratched" once or twice but he seemed
amidst perils and dangerous innumerable, to bear a
charmed life.

Willie came to the front as the war progressed and was

mustered in during January 1865. When he was just seventeen, he wore the gray. So that, with the exception of Allie, who was too young, I sent all my boys to the front, and my prayers went with them, and neither they nor I can ever be ashamed of the sense of honor which led them to battle for the Lost Cause. When the war was ended, the sentiment was unanimous in our family, that all the old issues had been settled, and that the result of the conflict was right.

The war over, July, 1865, George and Willie left home to attend the University of North Carolina, and afterwards the University of Virginia.

In 1865, Lewis A. Maverick and Ada Bradley were married. They settled on the Colorado near Austin.

Sam was with his regiment in North Carolina, when the war ended. He remained awhile at Pendleton, South Carolina, with his relatives, and returned to us.

Death of Lewis. Lewis became almost an invalid while attending the University of Vermont, and he was compelled for his health's sake to prosecute his studies at Chapel Hill, North Carolina, and in fact he was never quite well after his second winter in Burlington, Vermont. During the war he bore the seeds of disease visibly on his person and it made him quite unhappy at times to feel that the fatal malady was slowly but surely sapping his vigor, his youth, his life.

In the spring of 1866, his maladies developed rapidly, and it soon became evident that he could not live long.

No child was born of this union between Lewis and Ada. In 1870, Ada married Major Waelder, a prominent and much respected lawyer of San Antonio.

In September, 1869, George returned from college, and in October, 1869, Mr. Maverick took Mary to Staunton, Virginia, where she entered the Episcopal School of that place. Mary afterwards completed her studies in New York City at Mrs. Hoffman's School for young ladies.

Death of My Husband. Mr. Maverick was not strong or well in 1869, and it was upon our urgent request that

he went with Mary to Staunton, and the trip was of bene-
fit to him. He felt that the grave was not far distant, for
in the fall of 1869, he wrote his last will and testament;
but, while he saw that disease was making inroads upon
his strength, he would not heed the suggestions offered
by relatives or friends, cautioning him to remove his mind
from his cares and his business, and to seek rest and rec-
reation by travel, or in the curative properties of the
many springs in the Northern States. In the spring of
1870, Mr. Maverick became quite feeble—at last in August, he became much worse and we no longer had any
hopes of his recovery. Mr. Maverick breathed his last
on the 2nd day of September, 1870. I shall make no com-
ment here upon his pure and noble character, or upon the
tender feelings which lay deep in his heart—I comfort
myself with the sentiment that he is happy now in
the company of his beloved Agatha. . . . .

Since the death of my beloved husband, not a death
has occurred in our family. My five remaining children
have married happily, and I am now the mother of ten
children again. If Mr. Maverick were to look in upon us
today, he would be gratified at the good will, the good
health and the good fortune which have come and remained with us during the ten years past. I am thankful that God has spared me this long, to see my descendants all happy and prosperous—and I hope it will be
many years before the pleasant scene I am contemplating
shall be marred by misfortune or the hand of death.

Mrs Maverick

To look after your stock immediately or you will not have in eighteen months from this time one yearling nor calf to ten you now. It is said and that by some of our most respectable citizens that yearling and calves many hy seen by Dozing following and sucking your cows and branded in other peoples brands. While I am writing this I am informed that Morrison, Gove and Worcester have each written to Mr. Maverick on this same subject. But for fear that you are not afraid of it and hearing that Mr. Maverick is not in Texas to give you this information. In haste respectfully

A friend to justice

May - 1863

ANNONYMOUS LETTER SENT TO MRS. MAVERICK

The Term "Maverick".

What a pity to contradict The Century Dictionary, but the following letters tell a story of their own:

Extract from Letter Written for the St. Louis Republic.

St. Louis, Nov. 16 1889. In response to your request I herewith submit an account of the origin of the term "maverick", as applied to unbranded cattle.

Hon. Samuel A. Maverick, a citizen of San Antonio, Tex., was, during 1845, temporarily residing at Decrows Point, on Matagorda Bay. He was a lawyer with a strong propensity for speculation in real estate. In fact, all the enterprising men in Texas of that day went more or less wild over real estate at 5 and 10 cents per acre. An interesting volume could be written on the land craze of that period. During that year (1845) a neighbor being indebted to Mr. Maverick in the sum of $1,200 paid the debt in cattle, transferring 400 animals at $3 per head. Cattle were cheap in those days, the hides only being cashable in the foreign markets. Mr. Maverick did not want the cattle, but as it was a case of cattle or nothing, he passively received them and left them in charge of a colored family, nominally slave, but essentially free, while he and his own family returned to San Antonio. In the year of 1853 the cattle were removed from the Gulf coast to the Conquista ranch, on the east bank of the San Antonio river, 50 miles below San Antonio. Here as before, under the poor management of the colored family, who really were not to blame, as they had no interest in the outcome, the cattle were left to graze, to fatten, to multiply and to wander away. Mr.Maverick was absorbed in real estate and no doubt enjoyed the reflection that he was not encumbered by either the cattle or their managers.

About one-third of the calves were branded, and the branding-iron was kept so cold and rusty that in 1856 the entire plant or "brand" was estimated at only 400 head, the original number. To the ingenious minded the explanation will occur when it is stated that the branding of "mavericks" was perfectly "square" in those days, although the occupation had not been distinctly named.

Now the neighbors shrewdly surmised these calves to be Maverick's, and so they called them "mavericks"—but did they continue to recognize them as such? Ah no; they hastened to burn into their hides their own brands, and the beasts were Maverick's, "mavericks" no longer. The reader should bear in mind that before the day of fencing no owner could know his own cattle on the range except by the brand, and so the first brand settled the question of ownership. Thus the unbranded thray calves in those days were dubbed "mavericks," for they were most likely Maverick's, at least in that neck of the woods. The humorous neighborss who profited by Mr. Maverick's indirect liberality, thus jokingly gave him the credit for it and while they secured the profits he was permitted to acquire the experience.

The name took, and spread, for Texas was then the heart of the cattle industry of the United States. About the year 1856, Mr. Maverick sold the entire brand, 400 head, "as they ran," to Mr. A. Toutant Beauregard, a brother of the distinguished general. Mr. Beauregard, however, paid him $6 per head, and Mr. Maverick retired from the venture, thoroughly experienced against similar investments, but with an apparent profit of 100 per cent and the unique distinction of having his name bestowed upon a very dear friend of the human race. The truth is Mr. Maverick, was never a cattle king, for, with the exception of the herd mentioned and a few necessary cow ponies he never owned any cattle or horses.

To the stockmen of the West I submit this account and would remind them that of the thousand and one versions of the story only one can be correct. Be assured this is the true account.

George M. Maverick.

Matagorda 25th Novr. 1849

S. Maverick, Esq.,
   Dr. Sir,
            Your servant "Jack" has done me the honor to make me his amanuensis and requests that I inform you as follows, viz:

In the first place he sends his most dutiful regards to you and your family and says that his mother and self are quite well.

2nd.   He says that he is very anxious to see you as without assistance he finds it quite impossible to pen and brand your cattle on the Peninsula and the stock is consequently becoming more wild and unmanageable daily.

3rd.   He wishes to receive your approval of his marriage, which with your sanction he is anxious to consummate with a girl here called Elizabeth and owned by Miss Ward.

With best regards to self and family, I remain
Your humble servt.
John C. Graham

Port Lavaca, Sept. 3rd, 1850

Sam'l A. Maverick, Esq..
            Dear Sir,
                    Having just returned from the "Peninsula," Decrow's Point. I heard that your stock of cattle were all being lost or stolen from want of proper attention. This report so unfavorable to your interest induced me to suppose that you might wish or find it to your interest to dispose of said stock. I therefore address you this letter. If you wish to dispose of the balance of said stock I will offer you such a trade that I think you will conceive it be to your interest to make.

I have a tract of land lying in Washington County on the waters of Mill Creek six miles from Brenham, the County Seat, well timbered, well watered by the creek and springs and of the very best quality of soil (1/2 league) title warranted been in possession for the last ten years house and improvements and eighty acres under fence and in cultivation, rented now for $200 a year.

I will trade you this tract for a portion of the Peyton League on Peyton's Bayou and on such terms as I think will suit you. The reason I make this proposition is that I wish to go extensively into the stock raising business, horses, mules, and cattle, and I think if it should suit you that we could make such arrangements as would be mutually acceptable and profitable.

An early reply will oblige   ,

Your obdt. Servt.

James T. Lytle.

Matagorda, July 24th. 1852.

Mr. Maverick,

Dear Sir.

I am informed that you want to dispose of them cattle and place on the Peninsula. If such information should be correct, you will please state the price and terms of sale—they have been awfully neglected, not branded ever since you left, and will do you very little good, situated as they are.

Am, Sir Respectfully yours &.

James Stanley

To

Mr. Maverick,

San Antonio

Matagorda

Mrs.Mavric

Send someone to look after your stock of cattle immediately or you will not have in eighteen months from this time one yearling nor calf to ten cows. It is said and that by some of our most respectable citizens that yearlings and calves may be seen by dozens following and sucking your cows and branded in other people's brands.

While I am writing this I am informed that Morrison, Cove and Worcester have each written to Mr. Maverick on this same subject. But for fear that you are not apprised of it and hearing that Mr. Maverick is not in Texas, I give you this information.

In haste.

Respectffully,

A friend to Justice

May 1853

San Pedro, 18th July, 1856

Hon'ble. S. A. Maverick,

Austin.

Dear Sir,

Upon my reaching my "rancho" after our last interview, I called to see Jack two or three times, but not finding him at home, he being out gathering your stock, I presume, I finally sent him word by one of my negroes that you said "as soon as he would gather your cattle he should let me know." This message, by-the-bye, appears rather to have displeased the white man who received it, Jack being absent at the time. However this may be, Jack soon returned, and sent me word that he then had about 200 Hds. of your cattle in the range, and would comply with the

request as soon as he could make some drives. But as yet I have
received no message from him; and time slipping on fastly, I
find I will have to leave for Louisiana before having got through
with this matter. But my son will be here ready to receive your
cattle at any time, should my proposals prove acceptable to
you. From what your son, who procured him the pleasure of a
visit, told mine, (I being absent from home) Jack had on the
other day, as he said, about 200 again. Now I must conclude that
the negro boy is not over anxious that you should sell your stock,
either because he has there, indeed, an enviable birth, or because
he does not wish you to be convinced, by counting, of the gross
negligence of which he has been guilty. Under the circumstances,
I do not believe he will ever gather 300 heads. Therefore I will
make you the following proposals: to-wit: I will take the whole
stock as it now stands, and pay you for same, Two thousand
Dollars cash, provided you have disposed of no other beeves than
those taken by Capt. Walker. Or, I will pay you upon delivery,
Seven Dollars 25/100 per head. In either case, I should have the
exclusive use of your "jacal" & "coral", and of the premises from
Mr. Radaz' lower line, on the San Antonio River, down to the
mouth of the Marcelina for three years at least. Should any of
these proposals be agreeable, please inform my son of the same
by writing to "Leo J. Toutant, care of J. Twohig, Esq., San Antonio". Or by writing to myself to Bladon Springs, Alabama,
whither I am going.

I again repeat, Dr. Sir, what I said before: "that it is your interest to sell and mine to purchase". And the sooner the better.

With high respect, I remain, Sir,

Truly yours,

(Signed)   A.Toutant.

P. S. I understand that your men say we have branded two of
your calves. I have requested Mr. Whetstone to see into the matter, and if so, apply the proper remedy. Indeed I am surprised
that this has not happened more frequently, so little have your
cattle been attended to. The payment, if you accept, will be made
through the agency of my friend, J. Twohig, Esq. Please write
me word at Bladon Springs of the result of Mr. Thibodeaux's pe-
tition, which you had the kindness of taking charge.

For want of opportunity this letter has laid over several days, and
mailed only on my way down.

Austin, Texas, August 13th, 1856

Mr. Leo S. Toutant,

Dear Sir,

I rec'd a short time since from your
father a letter dated July 18, but which was mailed on his departure from Louisiana, in which he offered me seven dollars and
a quarter per head for my cattle at Conquista, or two thousand
for the lot without the difficulty and trouble of herding.

By last night's mail I have word that my negro boy is driven
away, and his life threatened, &c., so that I have now no power
to take care of the stock. Your Father wanted the corrals and
my land down to the Marcelina for at least 3 years. I judge the
cattle, my oxen, all the beeves (except 5 or 6 I sold to Capt.
Walker some months since) & 80 calves would be worth over 3
thousand. But situated as I am and considering the impossibility
of my attending to the business, I will now propose to you to

take all of said cattle and oxen on the premises and those which have strayed, at the sum offered by your father, provided you will consent to take and allow $250 for the wagon, yokes, hogs and horses,that are mine, and I am throwing in without rent a large tract and good corral &c. You know your father's wishes and can write me that you will take, or not, the whole affair at $2250, If so, it will be a finished trade between us. But if you do not wish to do so until you hear from your father, please write me a letter to that effect, and in the meantime it would result to the interest of your father and be greatly valued by me if you will send your herders around to gather up the stock and let it be understood you are buying them, so as to save them being run off by theives.

Please write and direct me at San Antonio, as I wish the letter to be recd. by my family. I address this to the care of Mr. Twohig by a direction in your father's letter.

Dear Sir, I remain
Yours truly &c.
(Signed)   S. A. Maverick

Rancho de San Pedro, Aug. 21st, 1856

S. A. Maverick, Esq.

Dear Sir,

I had the honor of receiving yesterday a letter from you dated the 13th inst. in which I see that you would be willing of accepting father's propositions, if he would consent at the same time to take in the sale your horses, hogs, &c. for $250.

Father having never mention to me of nothing else but of the offer that he had made to you that is to say $7 per head or $2,000 for the whole stock without excepting any. and at the same time to have the use of your corrals for three years.

It would be out of my power to give you a direct answer for your last proposition till I learn from him, though if you happen to make up your mind to let me have the cattle at his said price, I wish you would come down or send a responsible man when we would finish gathering to put your own brand on all those that Jack neglected to brand before we put ours on as it was father's direction when he started, and I shall bear the responsibility to take in, your horses, hogs, yokes and chains at a reasonable price, provided that some one delivers them to me as I do not know how many horses you have nor what they are! As for your hogs I have not perceive any of them for a very long time; the rest of your little things on the Rancho we would have no use for, principally of your wagon which is all rusty and rotten.

If you consent, please have the kindness to give me a direct answer so that we might commence the hardest work that we ever practiced.

I remain yours very respectfully,
Leo J. Toutant

LIFE AND CHARACTER OF SAMUEL AUGUSTUS MAVERICK
DELIVERED OCT. 1870 BEFORE THE
ALAMO LITERARY SOCIETY
BY GEO. CUPPLES M. D.

Samuel Augustus Maverick was born on the 28th of July, 1803, his mother being a daughter of General Robert Anderson, of South Carolina, of Revolutionary renown. Of Mr. Maverick's boyhood and youth little is known. Having received preliminary education in his own State, he entered Yale College, where he graduated. During his journeyings to and from Yale he made the acquaintance of one destined to be for long years his friend and neighbor, and to follow him to the tomb at an interval of but thirteen days. This was the late Wm. B. Jacques, who often spoke of the gravity and sedateness beyond his years of the young Maverick, whom he had first known in the morning of life.

At this time Mr. Maverick's friends looked forward to the time when he should become a leading man, and he himself was ambitious to excel and to take a political stand. But his views were diametrically opposed to the nullification ideas of the Carolinians, and he could not compromise with his opinions. He was not a disciple of Calhoun, through personally an admirer of the transcendent talent of that great statesman. Finding himself in politics directly at variance with all his neighbors, he left the State. An incident growing out of this difference had, no doubt, an important part in determining him to such a step as emigration, then much less common than now. His father on one occassion, after having answered Mr. Calhoun in a speech of great power, was made the subject of some intemperate remarks, which his son resented by challenging the utterer of them. In the encounter he wounded his antagonist, and afterwards nursed him until his recovery. Previous to this he had studied law under Henry St. George Tucker, at Winchester, Virginia, and had been admitted to practice at the bar of his own State.

He first moved to Alabama, and thence, in 1834, to Texas, arriving at San Antonio in 1835. In the fall of that year Messrs. Maverick, Jno. W. Smith and P. B. Cocke were arrested by Col. Ugartachia, commanding the Mexican troops who occupied the city. During their incarceration they contrived to keep up intelligence with Gen. Burleson, who commanded the Texan army then investing the town. On one occasion these three gentlemen were sentenced on suspicion to be shot, and were actually marched to the place of execution, when Mrs. Smith, now the wife of Mr. James B. Lee, living on the Medina, appeared on the ground, fell upon the earth, embracing the feet of the Mexican commander, begging piteously for a further investigation of their case. The investigation was finally granted, and resulted in the clearing of the prisoners, who were, however, kept under close guard. They made their escape, nevertheless, and joined the Texan army. Early on the moring of the 5th of December, 1835, Col. Ben. Milam attacked the city; S. A. Maverick as guide, with Milam at the head of the right division, moving down Soledad street to the LaGarza House—Johnson, commanding the left, marching down Acequia street to the same point, with Jno. W. Smith for guide. The cannon posted at the corner of the Main Plaza swept these streets. To procure water cur troops took the Veramendi House by digging a trench of five feet in depth across the street during the night of the fifth, and so going back and forth with heads bent to avoid the grapeshot. Of the seven hundred volunteers under Burleson

at the "Old Mill' above town, only two hundred fifty were under Milam—others joined them two days later, but the greater
number had gone home or to Goliad, where a force was then
gathering to move against Matamoras. On the 8th, Milam was
killed in the yard of the Veramendi House,* being shot through
the head; and by his side stood Mr. Maverick. On the 10th the
Mexicans ran up the white flag of surrender. The Texan troops
had fought incessantly night and day, and had taken all the
square block of buildings fronting the north side of the Main
Plaza, by digging through the walls of the houses from one to
another. Where the Plaza House now stands there lived the
priest, Padre Garza; from this house the Texans made a charge
and took and spiked the guns, the fire of which had been con-
centrated on that building and was fast crumbling it down. In
this charge Col. Ward lost a leg, and the young Carolinian, Bonham,
an eye. The Mexican gunners fled or were cut to pieces. This was
on the morning of the 10th, and was followed by the capitulation
of Gen. Cos, who was permitted to retire with his troops across
the Rio Grande.

Mr. Maverick's absence on March 6th, 1836, the day of the massacre of the Alamo, was due to his being sent a delegate to the
Convention of the people of Texas, in which capacity he, on the 2nd
day of March, signed the Declaration of Independence; the Hon. Jose
Antonio Navarro being the other delegate from the municipality
of Bexar, also present and signing.

After the battle of San Jacinto, the result of which secured
the safety of Texas, for a time at least, Mr. Maverick returned
to Alabama, where he married, in August of the same year, and
in 1838, returned to San Antonio with his family.

In March, 1842, Gen. Vasquez invaded western Texas entering
San Antonio with nine hundred men. On this occasion, Mr. Twohig
blew up his store to prevent the ammunition it contained from
falling into the hands of the enemy. The few American families
then living in San Antonio had made good their escape in time;
retiring to the Brazos river. The family of Mr. Maverick did not
return to San Antonio until 1847.

On the 12th day of September, of the same year, the District
Court being in session, a Mexican citizen, now dead, was visited
by some of his countrymen, known to be in the Mexican service;
from them he ascertained that Gen. Woll was close at hand
with a force of fourteen hundred men. This intelligence he com-
municated to Don Antonio Manchaca, who lost no time in making
it known to Judge Hutchinson. The few troops stationed in San
Antonio immediately withdrew, but the American citizens, with the
members of the bar, the presiding judge at their head, decided on
defending the place; Mr. Maverick, who was urgent in favor of this
course, declaring that they ought to set the example of resistance
and that whatever might be their fate, they would at least check
the advance of the enemy. and give time for succor to arrive from
the few and scattered settlements which existed at that day in

---

*This typical Spanish House, a quaint landmark until recent years, was the
home of Jean Martin Veramendi, vice-governor of Coahuila and Texas, elected
in 1830. Veramendi was known as a "man of liberal principles" and was
naturally friendly towards San Antonio since he was a resident. His daughter
married James Bowie one of the heroes of the "Alamo."
In 1835 Ben Milam was shot about twenty feet back of the Veramendi
home; S. A. Maverick who with Deaf Smith had guided the Texan forces into
the city, stood beside Milam and caught him in his arms as he fell dead.
A narrow street south of the Wolff and Marx store, Veramendi St., is all that
is left to mark this historic spot.

western Texas. They accordingly, in the night of Saturday, the 12th, took up their position on the flat roof of the building known as Maverick's, forming the corner of Commerce and Soledad streets, and commanding all the entrances to Main Plaza. The little band numbered fifty-three Americans and one Mexican, Mr. Manchaca, who had served through the War of Independence, from Bexar to San Jacinto, and was especially marked for vengeance by Santa Anna. Soon after daylight, in a thick fog, the Mexican troops entered the Main Plaza, music in front, little expecting the reception which awaited them. A pealing volley from the Texan rifles checked their march, and before Woll could withdraw them, fourteen were slain outright and twenty-seven wounded. Having placed his men under cover, Gen. Woll brought up two six-pounder guns, and being well advised of the numerical weakness of the Texans, made his disposition for surrounding them and cutting off their escape. On the roof of the Dwyer House, on the southeast corner of the Plaza, he posted thirty-five Cushatta Indians, who formed part of his force. Another detachment crossed the river and took post near the pecan tree, in front of the barracks. The east bank was guarded by Cavalry, also, and the preparations of the Mexican commander being now complete, he sent an officer, with a flag, to summon the little band to surrender as honorable prisoners of war, adding, that if the conditions offered were not accepted within ten minutes, he would advance on them with the bayonet. During the fire of musketry and artillery to which they were exposed while Woll was posting his troops, it is singular that not one of the little band of Texans was hit; they being partially covered by the low parapet of the flat-roofed house. The only one of them that received any injury was Mr. Manchaca, who was struck on the knee by a fragment of stone detached by a round shot— from the effects of which he walks lame to this day. Resistance being evidently vain, the small band surrendered, and were, on the retreat of Woll, marched to the Castle of Perote, and there imprisoned, under circumstances of the greatest harshness.

Gen. Woll has been generally and loudly denounced for breach of faith toward his prisoners; but it is not generally known that in sparing their lives he disobeyed the express orders of President Santa Anna, to put to death every man taken with arms in his hands as a rebel and a traitor. These orders were shown by Woll, in 1863, to an intimate friend of Mr. Maverick (now present) —on which occasion he made many friendly inquires for Maverick, Colquhoun, Twohig, and others, by name. When asked why he had not defended his course by the publication of these orders, Woll replied he himself owed, not only his life under similar circumstance, to the intervention of Santa Anna, but also his position in the Mexican army, and that he could not honorably vindicate himself by the exposure of one to whom he owed so much.

After the surrender of Maverick, Colquhoun, Twohig, Hutchinson, and their companions, Woll was utterly defeated with great loss, five miles from San Antonio, on the Solado, by the Texans under Hays and Burleson, and without loss on their own side, if we except the La Grange company, under Captain Dawson, which was surrounded by the Mexican troops in the prairie, while on march to rendezvous, and cut to pieces; seven only of their number escaping.

On the 23rd, Woll marched on his return to Mexico, carrying his citizen-prisoners with him. On the way, one of the number, Mr. Cunningham, died and was buried on the Leona. On their arrival at Perote they were subjected to the most humiliating and cruel treatment,beng confined to cells, and frequently chained two together; Major Colquhoun being, if I mistake not, Mr. Maverick's companion in these bonds of adversity. Of these they were relieved from time to time, to work on a stone quarry, or on the road which San Anna was constructing to his palace of Tacubaya. I have seen the quondam prisoners smile grimly when allusion was made to the little work the Mexicans got out of the Texan captives. While they were here many attempts were made to bribe them with promises of office and favor, and Mr. Maverick particularly, was approached, on account of his influence in Bexar; but he, like his companions in captivity, had naught but scorn for their offers, which utterly failed to seduce them from their faith and allegiance to Texas.

By the intercession of Waddy Thompson, then American minister to Mexico, and a relative of Mr. Maverick, the latter, with Judge Wm. E. Jones and old Judge Hutchinson, were released in April, 1843; others were released at the instance of the British minister; while others, of whom the leader was Jno. Twohig, disdained to ask protection from either power, and manfully dug their way out of the fortress, making good their escape to Texas, in the spring of 1844.

The following extract from a report of a speech made by Gen. Waddy Thompson, at Greenville, South Carolina, in May 1844, sets the conduct and character of Mr. Maverick during his captivity, in the most honorable light. "Amongst the many interesting "incidents which General Thompson mentioned, there was one "particularly so, as it related particularly to a gentleman born " and educated in this neighborhood—Mr. Samuel A. Maverick— "which, in the language of Gen. Thompson, was not only honor "able to the man himself, but to human nature. Mr. Maverick "was a young man of large fortune, with a young wife and three "or four interesting children. When he arrived at his prison, at "Perote, he wrote to General Thompson, informing him that he was "there and in chains, but said that he neither asked nor ex- "pected any interposition from Gen. Thompson, as he considered "that such interposition might not be proper, and only asking the "General to convey some letters to his family. Gen. Thompson "neverless, set about obtaining his release, and as there was then "a negotiation on foot for reannexation of Texas to Mexico, Gen. "Thompson wrote to Mr. Maverick, saying that if he was really in "favor of such reannexation, and would say so, he thought his "release would certainly be granted, as he, Gen. Thompson, would "say to Santa Anna that any promise which Maverick made would "certainly be complied with. Mr. Maverick replied: 'I regret that "I cannot bring myself to think that it would be to the interest "of Texas to re-unite with Mexico. This being my settled opinion, "I cannot sacrifice the interest of my country even to obtain my "liberty; still less can I say so when such is not my opinion, for "I regard a lie as a crime, and one which I cannot commit. Gen. "Thompson said that he felt a special pride in this heroic virtue "because Mr. Maverick was a South Carolinian, his neighbor, and "the 'kinsman of his kinsman.'"

I have dwelt at length on the history of the taking of San Antonio, and the adventures of the prisoners taken there, as they constitute the last episode of the Texas-Mexican war, of which San Antonio was the theatre, and they may give some idea of the danger and hardships to which the old Texans were exposed.

During his captivity, Mr. Maverick was elected by his fellow citizens of Bexar to the Senate. On his return, he found his family at La Grange, all sick; after removing them to the coast, near Decrows Point, he returned to South Carolina to procure means to meet obligations which he assumed in many instances for the relief of his more necessitous companions in captivity. He gradually sold his property elsewhere and invested in Texas lands. In 1847 he returned to San Antonio, where he continued to reside up to the time of his death, September 2nd of this year.

In 1838 he took out his law license in San Antonio. From 1838 until 1842 he was one of Hays' minute men, and often followed the trail of the marauding Indians under that celebrated chieftain. He accompanied his old leader, in 1848, on his expedition to open the route from San Antonio to El Paso del Norte. On this memorable trip they lost their way, and were at the point of starvation—one man actually perishing of hunger; when they were guided by Indians to San Elisario, on the Rio Grande, where they found food and rest. Their route back from El Paso established to brand mine...," but the following article and letters tell a story

In February, 1861, as one of the three Commissioners of the Committee of Public Safety, he was charged with the delicate duty of procuring the removal of the United States troops from the State of Texas—and that all this was effected without bloodshed, and with so little of inconvenience or humiliation to the officers and men who had so long been friends among us, constitutes one of his highest titles to the respect and gratitude of his fellow-citizens. and a very little acquaintance with the situation of af fairs at that time will satisfy any one, whatever views he may entertain on the question of secession, that but for this action of the Commissioners, civil war would have been inaugurated in the State; the Federal troops—numerous, well equipped and well commanded, forming a nucleus for an army composed of the forces which the Governor had already commanded to organize for the maintenance of Federal authority. No one who knows the feelings which prevailed throughout Texas can doubt that the Union army would soon have succumbed, but I repeat, that to the prudent yet energetic action of the Commissioners, and of their coadjutors, Texas owes it that no blood was shed within her borders, and that she escaped the horrors of war which devastated her sister States.

With this closed the public functions of Mr Maverick, which he had exercised in various capacities from the memorable day when he affixed his signature to the Declaration of Independence, and always with credit to himself and advantage to his constituents; his public services in either House, in conventions, or in any capacity whatever, being rendered with disinterestedness and freedom from all personal and party consideration; which, I trust, will yet from all personal and party considerations.

Truthful to a punctilio no man can say that he ever used equivocal language, and his sincerety was testified to by the confidence he commanded from all who knew him. And of those who enjoyed that privilege, who is there who does not remember to admire that courtesy of the old school which is fast passing away?

Prudent and considerate, he never said of the absent one word, which uttered in their presence, could have wounded or pained them. Modest and retiring to a fault he ever manifested that forgetfulness of his own comfort and convenience which is the true test of good breeding.

He was frugal and unostentatious in his habits, and he carried into practice his philosophic scorn of the gewgaws of fashion and of display. Years ago, when sickness and distress pressed hard on the poor classes in San Antonio, secretly, and as a thief in the night, Mr. Maverick came unto the then mayor of the city, bearing somethng under his cloak—that cloak which,¦ among the older inhabitants may be remembered as an historical relic—drawing forth the hidden object, Mr. Maverick, in his peculiar hurried manner, begged his honor to undertake the distribution among the necessitions of a thousand dollars, his contribution in this time of suffering, and above all, to say nothing of it.

To this Society he leaves the signal honor of having inscribed his name on the roll of its founders, and the task of rearing on the site, which you owe to his munificence, an edifice which may do honor to the donor and credit to your young Association, the Alamo Literary Society; a task in which I trust you will be aided by the wealthier members of the community.

To the inheritors of his name he has bequeathed a heritage richer than broad lands, more precious than fine gold—the name of a just, an upright and a conscientious man, of one who never compromised with his convictions, who never bowed the knee to expediency; and let them ever remember that the name they bear has long been a synonym for honor, integrity and truth.

SUBSTANCE COPY TO CAPT. COMDT. HOWE, SAN ANTONIO BEXAR

Capt. Comdt. S. M. Howe,
San Antonio, Bexar Co.

Port Cavallo, Matagorda Co., Tex.
July 3rd, 1847.

My dear Sir:—

I desire to make my excuses to Capt. Rawlins for not giving him a decisive answer in regard to some Alamo property, and as I am indebted to you for many civilities and you were the first to introduce the subject of the Goverment's supposed right to the same, I am going to beg of you the favor to say to Capt. Rawlins that the time intervening between our interview and my hurried departure from San Antonio was so short that I was unable to make any very extensive discoveries on the subject. But I did inquire of two or three of the old inhabitants, persons of information and veracty, who stated to me uniquivocally that the Alamo never was a fort, barracks, or anything of a Government post or military establishment but that it was a mission—"The Mission of San Antonio de Velero," like those missions below San Antonio and others over Mexico generally. It was enclosed in walls about 150 yards square in the first instance as a protection against wild Indians and afterwards given as a sort of uniform fashion for Catholic Indian Missions. These persons when questioned by me with regard to those uniform arches noticed by you and me on the West side, state with much plausibility (and no doubt truth) that these were the cells of the priests, etc. These arched buildings proclaim such a uniformity and unity of plan; but I think you gentlemen will agree with me that they belonged to no part of the plan of a fort. Being a Mission and having strong walls and contiguous stone houses caused it to be first used in 1835 and -6, etc. by the Mexican Military as a convenient place.

I was myself a prisoner in the hands of General Cos. in Dec. 1835 in San Antonio. Gen'l Cos' and Ugartechia's principal barracks were in the Military square in this city in 1835. Upon the approach of the first Texan army under Austin, Cos commenced putting the Alamo into fort fashion. During the month of November '35 with great labor, Cos for the first time turned the Alamo into a fort. He threw down the arches of the Church which now lie inbedded with the earth in order to make an inclined plane to haul cannon on top the Church. He also erected mounds at different distances on the sides for cannon. And being then a prisoner I do not positively know, but I am sure it was then or afterwards when Santa Anna massacred Travis & Co. that those bastions and other fort shapes were given to the Alamo.

My dear sir, I want you to bear me witness and I propose to submit the question to the careful investigation of Capt. Rawlins. But in making his inquiry there is only one thing to be guarded against, a two-complying or assentive disposition in the Mexicans (they do not like to say no, it appears to be a part of their politeness) I ask no favor, but I confidently look for justice. Though I must add that I have a desire to reside in this particular spot. A foolish prejudice, no doubt, as I was almost a solitary escape from the Alamo massacre having been sent by those unfortunate men only four days before the Mexican advance appeared, as their representative in the convention which declared Independence, etc. Capt. R. as a man of honor is aware of the immense advantage which the Government has in a contest with an individual. Let him in candor make the requisite inquires of the most respectable and disinterested old Mexicans. If they say that the Alamo was built for a fort I will freely surrender my supposed rights, but on the contrary if they say it was an old Mission and only accidently and recently used by the military merely because it was convenient, originally strong, etc., then I shall expect Capt. R. to withhold the strong arm of power from my poor privileges and my little predilections. If my proposition is not fair and equal, then I pray that you or Capt. R. will do me the favor to suggest some more acceptable plan of settlement. Forgive me, dear sir, and believe me, Your attached fellow citizen,

S. A. Maverick.

City of Houston,
September 2, 1839.

Samuel A. Maverick,, Esq.,
      San Antonio,
Dear Sir:—
              In compliance with the request of yourself and fellow citizens and my promise to do all for your relief in my power and which the exigencies of your situation demands, I have laid before His Excellency, the President, the Secretary of war and other offices of Goverment, the exposed and deplorable state of your frontier and your city in particular, and the result of my expositions and efforts are that Major Ross with his detachment of about seventy men, well mounted and well armed, has been ordered to include your section of country in his circuit of ranging and to afford you all the protection in his power. The President has also written individually to John H. Moore on the Colorado to raise two hundred men to range out your way. No force can for the present be made stationary at your place, although this will be attended to as soon as recruits may be had from the United States.

I write this in consummate haste as the gentleman who takes

this is on horse awaiting. Our friend I. P. Borden is at my elbow and sends his best respects to you and his thanks for the documents which you remitted to him by me.

With the assurances of my esteem and regard for yourself and all our friends,

I, Sir, remain, Yours obediently,
Thomas G. Western

Seguin, 26, February 1842.

Dear Sirs:

There are a number of our citizens who feel desirous to render you such aid as may be in our power in case of an attack upon your city. You will, therefore, oblige us by giving us information by return mail, and at all times when you think prudent, of your situation, and we will depend upon your information and act according to your advice. We have many rumours here and know not truly what to believe, and the people generally are busily employed, and they do not wish to act until necessity requires, so that my giving us correct information, we will depend upon it and come out to your aid if really needed.

We understand that an express went on yesterday morning to Gonzales for aid. Why not give us the news also? And we can render you some aid and forward the express to the next settlement. A company will leave this in one or two hours notice for Bexar on foot at any time, so that we may be relied on when you send for us by giving us the true situation of your affairs, and we will not encumber ourselves unnecessarily by horses or anything else but arms, and can march through in a night.

Be particular to write by mail if possible.

I am, gentlemen,
Your obedient servant,
A. Neill

Messrs. C. Van Ness
Ed Dwyer and S. A. Maverick

---

gal one Maverick 4 30 Hill

MRS DICKINSON'S STORY OF THE "FALL OF THE ALAMO."

Mrs. Dickinson told Dean Richardson of St Marks Episcopal Church the following story of the "Fall of the Alamo", several times; once when the transfer of the Alamo property from the Church to the State was about to be made (1883). At this time, she walked with him and a party of others to an inner room in the Alamo, and pointed it out as the one in which she and the Mexican women were asked to stay, and where they were when the Alamo fell.

The first attack of the Mexicans was over, and all seemed peaceful, when one day Lieutenant Dickinson came hurriedly up to their home on Main Plaza, saying:

"Give me the baby; jump on behind me and ask me no questions."

They galloped down to the crossing, at the point where the "Mill Bridge" now is, but not in time to escape being fired at by the incoming Mexicans: however, they succeeded in crossing and hastened over to the Alamo.

Mrs. Dickinson said she saw no fighting—only the noise of the battle reaching her and the few Mexican women inside the Alamo.

On the day of the fall, Sunday, her husband kissed her good-bye in the morning, and she never saw him again.

Probably she and the Mexican women, who were her companions, saw the bayoneting of the last American; when the shooting was over, a soldier crawled into the room where they were, not to seek refuge, but to carry out an order previously given, and generally understood, which was that if the garrison fell someone was to try to fire the powder supply; and this man named Evans, wounded and spent with weariness, was killed while making his painful way to the powder room.

One of the Mexican officers, always thought by Mrs. Dickinson to be General Almonte, Chief of Staff to Santa Anna, who spoke broken English, stepped to the door of the room in which the women were, and asked:

"Is Mrs Dickinson here?"

As she feared to answer and kept quiet, he repeated:

"Is Mrs. Dickinson here? Speak out, for it is a matter of life and death."

Then she answered, telling who she was, and he took her in charge over to Main Plaza. Here she and her child were held and cared for some days, when she was given a horse and a bag of provisions and told to go. She and her baby and a colored man-servant journeyed safely eastward to the town of Washington, then the Capital, where she lived some years, later returning to visit in San Antonio.